THE FOOD OF MYANMAR

Authentic Recipes from the Land of the Golden Pagodas

Recipes by **Claudia Saw Lwin Robert**
Introductory articles by **Wendy Hutton**, **San Lwin** and **Win Pe**
Photography by **Luca Invernizzi Tettoni**

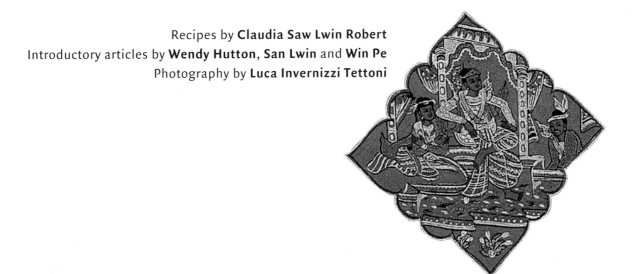

TUTTLE Publishing

Tokyo | Rutland, Vermont | Singapore

Contents

Part One: Food in Myanmar

The undiscovered treasures of the Land of Gold are its culinary gemstones.

By Wendy Hutton

The food of Myanmar, "The Land of Gold" of ancient Indian and Chinese manuscripts, is one of the least known Asian cuisines. This is more a result of the country's period of self-imposed isolation than the intrinsic quality of the food itself. However, as Myanmar—or Burma as it was previously called—opens its doors to visitors and international business, more people are discovering its intriguingly different cuisine.

Sitting between India and China, two powerful nations with strong cultural traditions, and sharing borders with Bangladesh, Laos and Thailand, Myanmar's beginning dates back some 2,500 years, when Tibeto-Myanmarn-speaking people moved from Tibet and Yunnan into the northern part of the country. Kingdoms rose and fell over the centuries, many different tribes arrived and established themselves, and various Western powers set up coastal trading posts.

The British gained control over the country little by little, annexing it to British India, until the last king was dethroned in 1886. Myanmar regained its independence in 1946, becoming a socialist republic in 1974. In 1979, the ruling authorities changed the name to Myanmar.

Once known for its vast wealth in teak, rubies, jade and rice, Myanmar has in recent times set about developing into a modern nation. Yet it is the glittering golden stupas, the stone remains of ancient kingdoms, the timeless movement of wooden boats along the giant Ayeyarwady (Irrawaddy) River, the bustle and colour of local markets and the charm and gracious generosity of its people which remain in the visitor's mind long after departing.

Owing to the prevalence of Chinese, Indian, Thai and Western restaurants in tourist hotels, some visitors leave Myanmar without experiencing the local cuisine. Full of flavour, healthful, sometimes hauntingly similar to neighbouring cuisines, at other times dramatically different, the food of Myanmar is not complex to prepare at home.

Based on rice with a range of tasty side dishes, salads, soups and condiments, Myanmar cuisine offers a wide choice of flavours. Although the vast majority of the population is Buddhist, they make a distinction between taking life and buying food which has already been caught or killed. In general, Myanmar's Muslims slaughter the cattle and catch fish, while pigs are reared by the Chinese.

French gourmet Alexander Dumas once remarked that the discovery of a new dish was as important as the discovery of a new constellation. How much more exciting, then, to discover an almost unknown cuisine. The food of Myanmar awaits you.

Page 2:
The magnificent ruins of Bagan (Pagan) date back to the 11th and 12th centuries.
Opposite:
Dining by the timeless Ayeyarwady (Irrawaddy) River, Myanmar's main waterway which was referred to by Kipling as the "road to Mandalay".

From the Delta, Plains and Mountains

Myanmar's dramatically varied terrain offers a range of regional flavours.

By Wendy Hutton and San Lwin

"Burma . . . is peopled by so many races that truly we know not how many . . . in no other area are the races so diverse, or the languages and dialects so numerous ...". Thus wrote C.M. Enriquez in *Races of Burma* in 1933. Although religion and tribal customs influence the cuisine of the people of this polyglot land—in which today's specialists have identified 67 separate indigenous groups—it is perhaps the terrain and climate which have had the greatest effect on regional cuisines. These factors determine the basic produce and therefore influence the dishes prepared by the people living in each area.

The Myanmarese tend to classify their country into three broad areas: what used to be referred to as "Lower Burma", the humid Ayeyarwady delta around Yangon, and the land stretching far south into the Isthmus of Kra; "Middle Burma", the central zone around Mandalay, ringed by mountain ranges and thus the driest area in all of Southeast Asia, and "Upcountry", the mountainous regions which include the Shan Plateau and Shan Hills to the east, the Chin Hills to the west and the ranges frequented by the Kachin tribe to the far north.

The long southern coastal strip of "Lower Burma", Tanintharyi, is washed by the waters of the Andaman Sea and shares a border with Thailand. This region is rich in all kinds of seafood, which is understandably preferred to meat or poultry. While people in other areas of Myanmar eat freshwater fish caught in the rivers, lakes and irrigation canals, this coastal region offers a cornucopia of marine fish, crabs, squid, prawns, lobsters, oysters and shellfish.

Myeik, the main southern port (once known as Mergui) is an important centre for dried seafood such as shrimp, fish and jellyfish, as well as for the precious birds' nests made from the saliva of two varieties of swiftlet. Bird's nest, however, does not form part of the local diet but is traded—as it has been for centuries—with the Chinese for sale in traditional medicine shops and food stores.

Dishes from the lowland southern region are more likely to include coconut milk than those

Opposite: Fishermen on the picturesque Inle Lake drop large traps over shoals of fish before spearing them through a hole in the top of the cage.
Left: A Rakhine woman dries rice crackers in the sun.

of other areas of the country. For example, the southern version of the banana leaf packets of chopped seasoned pork typical of central Myanmar and the Shan Hills contains fish rather than pork, and is enriched with coconut milk rather than stock.

Flowing in a general north-south direction for some 2,170 kilometres, the life-giving Ayeyarwady rises in the mountains of the far north, then branches into a maze of rivers and creeks that make up the delta— about 270 kilometres at its widest. This is the rice granary of the nation. Rice is the staple crop in Myanmar and is consumed not only for the main meals of the day but for snacks as well. It is eaten boiled, steamed and parched; in the form of dough or noodles; drunk as wine or distilled as spirits. The quality of the rice cultivated ranges from the stout, reddish kernels of the swidden plots to the slender, translucent grains favoured in many parts of the Shan State. Of the 8 million hectares of cereal crops under cultivation, rice accounts for 7½ million of these; the remainder is devoted to maize, wheat, millet and other cereal crops, cultivated for both the domestic and export markets. Oil crops such as sesame, sunflower and niger seeds are produced almost exclusively for domestic use.

Opposite: The weekly floating market at Ywama village, Inle Lake, is a colourful affair.
Right: Farmers sell turnips wholesale to middlemen and traders.

A combined coastal length of about 2,400 kilometres and a network of rivers, irrigation channels and estuaries, particularly in the Ayeyarwady delta region, yields a dazzling array of fresh- and saltwater fish, lobsters, prawns, shrimp and crabs. The Ayeyarwady delta supplies the bulk of freshwater fish, sold fresh, dried, fermented or made into the all-important *ngapi*, a dried fish or shrimp paste (similar to Thai *kapi*, Malaysian *belacan* and Indonesian *trasi*). Not surprisingly, people living in this region also make abundant use of dried shrimp as a seasoning for soups, sauces, salads and countless other dishes.

To the west of the Ayeyarwady is its most important tributary, the Chindwin River. This river flows along the Chin Hills which form a natural border between Myanmar and India and which are the source, not only of fine apples, but also the smooth-textured, sweet and tender meat of a species of half-wild, free-ranging cattle called gayal or mithun. In general, though, cattle and water buffaloes are raised as draught animals rather than for consumption.

East of the Chindwin-Ayeyarwady confluence, a trio of rivers race down from the Shan Plateau to the Ayeyarwady, where they are harnessed to a system of weirs and canals constructed in the 11th century to allow multicrop-

ping. Further east, the mighty, rumbustious and mostly unnavigable Thanlwin rises in China, eventually pouring into the Andaman Sea. The Sittaung has its mouth a little further west of the Thanlwin and flows into the Bay of Martaban. Market gardens spring up on its alluvial banks after the monsoon has retreated and freshwater fisheries are set up along its drainage area.

Arakan, now known as Rahkine, is a flat strip of land facing the Bay of Bengal on the west coast of Myanmar, sharing its northern border with Bangladesh. The people of this once proud, independent kingdom have traded with Indian merchants for centuries, and a certain amount of inter-marriage has left its mark in their skin colouring, which is darker than that of most Myanmarese. Although the majority of Rakhines are Buddhist, there is a sizable population of Muslims of Bengali descent who work as fishermen (something no devout Buddhist would do as it means taking life). Islam prohibits the eating of pork, and the cuisine of Arakan's Muslims is perhaps closer to that of neighbouring Bangladesh than to other areas of Myanmar.

Tuna, sardines, grouper, sharks, stingrays, oysters, mussels, prawns, shrimp, softshelled crab, sea cucumbers and even jellyfish, processed into think gelatinous slices, are harvested from this coastal strip, famous for its extensive beaches such as Ngapali, named after the well-known resort city of Naples. Touted as an aphrodisiac, the heart of sea urchins served chilled on squares of cucumber is relished in Ngapali. The eating of saltwater fish was only accepted by the majority of people as recently as 30 years ago; prior to that they were accustomed only to the taste of freshwater fish. Loach, featherback, hilsa, barb and freshwater catfish are preferred, while large fish such as sheatfish, giant sea perch and large river catfish are usually sold in cuts. This preference for smaller fish has its roots in the Buddhist dislike of eating large animals.

Mandalay, where the last king of Burma ruled, is the cultural heart of the fiercely hot, dry plains of central Myanmar. Irrigation has made it possible to expand agriculture from dry rice (which de-

A duck farmer tends to his flock by boat on the Ayeyarwady River at Amarapura.

countries, and to a strong Chinese element in the population, but by terrain and climate. A wide variety of foods is grown here: rice, wheat, soya beans, sugar cane, niger seed, sunflowers, maize and peanuts; and vegetables including potatoes, cabbage, cucumber, cauliflower, celery, eggplant, hops, kale, kholrabi, lettuce, mustard, rape, roselle, tomatoes and chayote. Fruit from the Shan Plateau and the Kachin Hills includes oranges, tangerines, quinces, damson plums, peaches, pomegranates, persimmons, pears and strawberries. In Myanmar generally, the indigenous tropical and temperate flora has been supplemented by exotics such as the pineapple, tomato, chilli, tobacco, grapefruit, apple, loquat, lychee, sapodilla, sweetsop, soursop and rambutan.

Fish seldom features on local menus, unless it is dried fish or unless one happens to be in the region of Inle Lake, where freshwater fish is caught. There is a famous composite dish from this area called Kneaded Shan Rice (page 46) which is based on rice mixed with cooked freshwater fish, onion and seasonings, pressed into shape and decorated with fried chilli, spring onions, and pieces of crisp, deep-fried buffalo skin.

The Shan are known for their love of pork, and also eat more beef than most other people in Myanmar. However, in Myanmar's more impoverished mountainous regions, all kinds of esoteric items

pended on seasonal rain for its growth) to include crops such as peanut, sorghum, sesame, corn and many types of bean and lentil. Various fermented bean or lentil sauces and pastes are used as seasonings in this region, rather than the fermented fish and shrimp products typical of the south.

Not having access to fresh seafood, the people of the central plains generally eat freshwater fish, with the occasional dish of pork or beef. One famous dish from this region is known as "Pork Packets". Finely chopped, seasoned pork is steamed in a banana leaf wrapper and served with a dip of crisp fried garlic, chilli powder, vinegar, salt and sugar.

The most populated "upcountry" area of Myanmar is the Shan Plateau, a region of mountain ranges and wide fertile valleys with a mean altitude of 1,050 metres above sea level, adjoining China, Laos and Thailand. Food preferences here are influenced not only by proximity to these such as ants, grasshoppers, dragon-flies and insect larvae are eaten. The Shan and other tribes living in mountainous regions are more likely to use a wide range of wild greens gathered from shrubs and forests rather than vegetables cultivated in fields.

Soups from this region are more likely to be based on beef or pork stock than made with fish or dried shrimp. The soups are not as clear as those found elsewhere in Myanmar, as they are often thickened with powdered soya bean. One example of this is the Shan version of Myanmarese noodles (*kyaukswe*), which is based on pork in a soup thickened with powdered soya bean, rather than made with chicken and coconut milk as in the rest of the country.

The hill rice grown on the Shan Plateau and in other upcountry regions is renowned for its variety and flavour, and unlike the rice of the central and lower regions, depends on seasonal rain rather than irrigation. Glutinous rice, however, is the preferred staple in much of the Shan country, as it is in neighbouring Laos and northeast Thailand.

All kinds of beans and lentils are grown in the Shan Plateau. They are not only eaten whole for protein, but are also fermented to make a seasoning paste, similar to the sauce made from lentils in central Myanmar.

Such products replace the fish-based seasonings, such as *ngapi*, or fermented pressed fish and

A farmer winnows paddy in the Shan Plateau. Rice is the staple crop in Myanmar.

dried shrimp, which are found in the lowland coastal areas and delta region. The Shan tribes also make a fermented soya bean product similar to the Indonesian *tempe*, which is often dried, pounded and used as a seasoning.

Given this wealth of food products, it is not surprising that there were times in Myanmar's history when the king could demand and receive three hundred different dishes for every meal. This extravagant practice was ended in the 19th century by the pious King Mindon, patron of Buddhism's Fifth Great Council, who reduced the number of dishes to a modest one hundred. However, with the dismantling of the centrally planned socialist economy—resulting in the mushrooming of private agribusinesses, livestock farms and seafood farms—supermarkets in Myanmar will soon be displaying products far more varied than ever could have been imagined by the royal chefs of old.

A Complex Culinary Mosaic

Poised between India, China and Southeast Asia, Myanmar has developed its own unique cuisine.

By Wendy Hutton

Surrounded by India and Bangladesh to the northwest, China to the northeast, and Laos and Thailand to the southeast, Myanmar has inevitably been influenced by the culture and cuisine of its neighbours. Yet despite the proximity of these countries, as well as large-scale migration of Indians and Chinese during the British colonial period, the cuisine of Myanmar offers a unique range of dishes which deserves to be more widely known.

China has had a marked impact on the food of Southeast Asia, including that of Myanmar. This is especially true in terms of ingredients, which have now been thoroughly absorbed into the local cuisine. Noodles made from wheat, rice and mung peas are perhaps the most noticeable legacy of China. In Myanmar, these are found in noodle soups like *mohinga*, a spicy, fish-based dish with sliced banana heart that is virtually the national dish. Another widely available dish is chicken in spicy coconut gravy, *ohn-no kyaukswe*, which includes either wheat, rice or mung pea ("transparent") noodles.

The soya bean, a native of China, appears in many guises in Myanmar: soy sauce; fermented soya beans (sometimes pressed into a cake and dried) and beancurd. Taking their cue from the Chinese, the Shan people near the border create a unique beancurd using chickpeas. Beansprouts, so popular in China, are made from several type of beans including soya beans and mung peas; they are eaten fresh or left to ferment and eaten as a salad or condiment. Sesame seeds and dried black mushrooms are other frequently used Chinese ingredients. Chinese preserved sweet and sour fruits, such as tamarind, mango, Indian *jujube* and plum, are favourite snacks, although those made in Myanmar tend to be sourer than their Chinese counterparts and contain chilli to cater to local tastes.

The Indian influence on Myanmar food is seen in the widespread use of ingredients such as

Opposite: Savoury coconut rice, a Mon dish of yellow rice topped with catfish, and Fried Rice with Peas are just three examples of rice dishes served in Myanmar. *Left:* Shan, Padaung and Pa-O people sell their wares at a colourful hilltribe market which rotates between five towns in the Shan State.

chickpeas, coriander seeds, cumin and turmeric. But whereas Indian cuisine relies on a complex blending of spices, Myanmarese food uses only a few dried spices, adding extra flavour with many fresh seasonings and condiments. Although chickpeas are eaten whole and made into a flour (*besan*), which is often used in batters, they appear most frequently in Myanmarese cuisine in the form of a nutty-tasting condiment, made by roasting and grinding the chickpeas to a powder.

Pungent curry leaves, popular in southern Indian cuisine, are used in some areas of Myanmar, as is the "drumstick", the seed pod of the horseradish or Moringa tree, eaten as a vegetable (in other parts of Southeast Asia, only the leaves are eaten).

Opposite: Introduced by the Chinese, noodles made from rice, wheat or mung peas are often used in "salads" and meal-in-one snacks bought from hawker stalls.

Owing to the presence of a considerable number of people of ethnic Indian origin in Rangoon (Yangon) and, to a lesser extent, in other major towns, Indian foods such as griddle-baked breads and almost achingly sweet cakes are widely available and popular with the Myanmarese. A popular Indian cake of semolina cooked with raisins is also made by the Myanmarese, although with a local touch in the form of coconut milk.

The food of Myanmar has, perhaps, more in common with its Southeast Asian neighbours, Laos and Thailand, than with India. The use of fermented shrimp and fish products such as dried paste, fermented fish in liquid, and clear fish sauce has parallels in both Laos and Thailand, where these ingredients largely replace salt and give a characteristic flavour to many dishes.

The sour fruit of the tamarind tree, most commonly used in the form of a dried pulp, is often preferred to vinegar or lime juice in many Myanmarese dishes. Fragrant lemongrass, the intensely perfumed kaffir lime leaf and galangal (a type of ginger) which give a wonderful aroma to so many Thai dishes are also popular in the southern region of Myanmar.

One passion which Myanmarese share with the people of Thailand and Laos is the love of a huge range of raw vegetables and leaves, both cultivated and wild, eaten with a pungent dipping sauce—a custom unknown in India or China. Myanmarese cooks have developed a range of dipping sauces, most of which contain chilli and are based around some form of dried or fermented shrimp. Soups, too, feature at virtually every main meal in Myanmar, as they do in Laos and Thailand.

Palm sugar, produced from the sap of the inflorescence of the aren palm, is another ingredient shared with Laos and Thailand, as is the preference for glutinous or "sticky" rice in parts of Myanmar bordering on these countries. Coconut milk, so prevalent in the cuisine of Southeast Asia, is also used in many Myanmarese dishes and for sweetmeats, while agar agar—a setting agent from seaweed—is also popular in Myanmarese desserts and drinks.

As with the people of Laos and Thailand, Myanmarese cooks frequently use pieces of banana leaf to wrap food before steaming—a technique not found in India.

Poised between two culinary giants, India and China, and inspired by the ingredients and styles of Southeast Asia, the cuisine of Myanmar has developed a unique personality of its own.

Festive Rice

When it comes to food for special occasions,
the humble rice grain turns up in delicious new ways.

By San Lwin

Buddhism permeates every aspect of life in Myanmar and each of the twelve lunar months on the Myanmarese calendar is associated with at least one religious festival. In addition, there are special festivities and holidays associated with secular occasions and pre-Buddhist festivals such as the Taungbyon Nat festival, a week-long celebration with music, drinking and dance held near Mandalay. And in a land where the question "Have you eaten?" serves as a form of greeting, most festivals are celebrated with feasting. On these occasions, everyday fare is put aside in favour of special treats served only at the time of the festival, each of which is of particular significance. And, as befits the food which provides the basis of almost every meal, it is rice, prepared in a variety of ways, that is one of the main culinary attractions at every festival.

The first month of the year, Dagu, which usually begins somewhere in April, marks the time of transition into the new year. It is also the hottest time of the year. So, with temperatures soaring, the water festival is held, as it is in other Buddhist nations of Southeast Asia such as Thailand and Laos. Merrymaking is the order of the day: there is singing, dancing and, of course, water—sprinkled piously on images of Buddha and vigorously splashed, sprayed and thrown over everyone else.

Dotted here and there among all this good-humored uproar are quiet circles of girls and women. Sitting around boiling pots of water, either in festive pavilions or at home, the womenfolk roll balls of rice dough, shred coconut meat into thin threads and, of course, gossip. Now and then a score or more of dumplings are tipped from a plate into the boiling water where they sink down for a few moments, only to bob up again on the surface, at which point they are retrieved with a colander, arranged on a plate, dressed with shredded coconut and served to guests. As the guests enjoy the small dumplings stuffed with palm sugar, covert glances are cast at them by those sitting around the boiling pot. A few of the dumplings have been stuffed with hot green chillies and, at the sight of the unwary victim whose tongue is on fire having bitten into one of these sabotaged dumplings, the women burst into appreciative giggles.

Also served during the New Year period is Thingyan rice. The rice is cooked in an earthenware pot which has been treated with beeswax fumes to impart a special fragrance. The rice is served steeped in cool water and accompanied by dishes of smoked, dried fish dressed in sesame

Opposite: *Nobody escapes a drenching during the water-throwing festival, or Thingyan, in Mandalay.*

oil, and a sweet and sour salad made of chopped *marann* plums. The *marann* is a succulent, acutely sour fruit related to the mango. This tradition goes back to the days of Burmese monarchs when Thingyan rice was served ceremoniously to the king and chief queen as they sat on the Bee Throne in the Glass Palace in Mandalay.

Another special festival rice is the treacly Htamane rice made during the month of Dabaung, which comes just before the month of Dagu and is the time when the harvest of new rice is plentiful. This treacly rice is a rich concoction of glutinous rice, sesame seeds, peanuts and slices of ginger and coconut; the mixture is stirred continuously while being cooked in water with lashings of sesame oil. Preparation of this delicacy sometimes takes the form of a friendly competition. Groups of contenders jostle around giant woks—the menfolk wielding spatulas big enough to paddle canoes with which to stir the rice—while sparks stream out from the wood fires tended by women waving fans. The merry sounds of tootling flutes, throaty oboes and stuttering double-headed drums, accented by the rythmic beat of bamboo clappers, accompany the activity. The musicians encourage the stirrers to turn out the tastiest, creamiest treacly rice in the minimum amount of time. This custom can be traced

Opposite: Towering fruit cakes are made by steaming a mixture of palm sugar, raisins, coconut milk and finely ground rice. Right: Young dancers performing at the State School of Music and Drama in Mandalay.

back to the Second Inwa Period during the 18th century. Historical accounts describe how troopers of the royal cavalry, under the supervision of the minister of the granaries, prepared one thousand pots of the rice. This rice was then donated to the monasteries and pagodas by the king, as custom decreed.

As is the case in most agricultural societies, the harvest festival in Myanmar holds great significance and is celebrated by those living in the lowlands as well as by the people of the hills. From this practice of celebrating the "eating of the new rice" comes the preparation of *mounh zann*, or new rice flakes, which can either be eaten fresh or kept for months. Ears of glutinous rice are collected when they are just ripe and the grains are roasted right after threshing. The roasted grain is pounded lightly in a mortar with a lightweight pestle, husked and, after the chaff has been removed, the rice flakes are either stored for consumption at a future time or, if they are to be eaten soon, kneaded with sugar and coconut shreds after being sprinkled with hot water.

Whatever the celebration, the preparation and consumption of dishes for special occasions will always be a part of the activities that constitute such a strong part of the Myanmarese identity and which continue to affirm community bonds.

Traditional Meals

*Courteous manners, generosity and a wide variety of dishes
are all part of the Myanmarese meal.*

By San Lwin

Breakfast in Myanmar is traditionally a light repast of fried rice, or yesterday's rice warmed up, served with boiled garden peas and green tea. Many delicious alternatives are now becoming popular though. Breakfast today could take the form of steamed glutinous rice topped with roasted sesame seeds and fish or vegetable fritters; smoked dried fish; *mohinga*, thin rice noodles in fish soup; or *ohn-no kyaukswe*, wheat flour noodles in chicken and coconut gravy. Rice gruel garnished with chunks of fried Chinese dough sticks might be gulped down, as might *naan*, flat bread fresh from the *tandoor* oven, with either boiled garden pea salad or lamb bone soup. Alternatively, a steaming chickpea broth or a chicken curry might provide the morning's sustenance. Coffee or tea sweetened with sugar and milk have become fashionable and are now common in most homes, replacing the simple green tea.

For main meals, the family gathers around a Western-style dining table with chairs. Once the family meal would have been eaten from the traditional dining table, a vast lacquered tray on a low stand, and big enough to accommodate the dishes for the whole family. Family members would sit on the floor around the tray, the men cross-legged and the women sitting modestly sideways. Deferential treatment towards one's parents is still observed. A father's place is at the head of the table with his wife on his left and eldest son on his right, the eldest daughter to the left of his wife and the rest of the brood seated in that fashion.

The meal is not served in courses as in the West. All the dishes, soups, condiments and vegetable dips are arranged in the middle, with a large bowl of rice for second helpings placed on the side. The children must wait patiently, stomachs grumbling, until the father and then the mother have taken some of the curry before serving themselves. Should the father be detained on urgent business, a choice morsel of the meal is placed on his plate as an act of obeisance. No wine or liquor accompanies the typical meal for a family and, with soup present on most occasions, liquid refreshment such as water or tea is usually reserved for the end of the meal.

Rice provides the bulk of the meal and the type of rice served may vary according to regional preference. Even freshly cooked plain rice is sometimes given an extra soupçon of flavour by covering it with fragrant screwpine (*pandan*) leaves which impart a delicate fragrance to the rice. Following the Buddhist tradition of acquiring merit, rice offered as a gift to monks is usually prepared in this way as it is considered an honour to serve food to a monk.

Meat and fish dishes are usually prepared in the form of curries, with fish dishes being much more popular in the lands bordering the lower reaches of the Ayeyarwady River and the delta region, while upcountry palates are partial to beans and pulses and their various by-products. Most curries are prepared with a thin gravy, which is then drizzled over the rice, mixed in and eaten with the fish or vegetables and fish preserve.

Soup is almost always served during the course of a meal and helps wash down the rice. It may be either a *hingga*, meaning a hot peppery soup, or a *hincho*, a slightly milder concoction. The soup is usually a clear broth with leaves, buds or slices of fruit. On more formal occasions, a thicker broth of fish and vegetables is served with rice noodles.

Vegetable and fruit salads are very popular as side dishes and provide an opportunity for the home cook to exhibit his or her creativity. The base of a salad might be prawns, sliced chicken, pork intestine, goat ear, fish in brine, or any one of a number of leaves, buds, fruits and herbs that can be found in Myanmar. Ingredients such as sliced onion, crushed garlic, shrimp paste, dried shrimp powder, ground peas, peanut or sesame oil are all thoroughly mixed by hand, not just tossed and served. Some of the heavier salads, such as a rice-based "salad", can be eaten either as snacks between meals or as meals in themselves. A rice-based salad might include rice mixed with chilli cooked in oil, slices of boiled potato, flour noodles, glass or thread noodles, beancurd, grated green papaya, pounded dried shrimp, pea powder, crisp-fried garlic and any other ingredient, all mixed together thoroughly.

Lunch for Pa-O minority farmers outside Kalaw on the edge of the Shan Plateau.

No meal would be complete without the condiment *ngapi*, or to use its full name, *ngapi-seinsa*: fish, or sometimes shrimp, boiled and garnished with crushed garlic, toasted dried chillies and chilli powder. Used as a dip for fresh, boiled or pickled vegetables and fruit, it forms the heart of Myanmarese cuisine and, for its aficionados, makes a complete meal in itself when poured liberally over steaming rice. Used in a variety of ways, it is best

toasted to an aromatic turn and either made into a salad with onions, garlic, green chilli and drenched in the juice of a lime, or pounded together with dried shrimp, onions, garlic and powdered chilli and formed into a ball, from which bits are scraped off and eaten with thin slices of lime or vegetables. It is used to flavour fish and certain vegetable dishes, but rarely chicken or meat. Most people buy it from the market rather than making it at home.

In the mountainous regions of the north and east, the Shan and Kachin States, fermented and dried soya bean takes over the crown from *ngapi*. It comes in many forms: from thick round balls or cylinders which are usually roasted before being pounded or shredded and fried with garlic and dried chilli, to thin sheets which are toasted over a fire and dressed with oil and salt. It is sometimes made into beancurd, as are green peas and chickpeas.

After a meal, fruits such as banana, mango, pomelo and durian are usually eaten in lieu of cooked desserts, which tend to be eaten as snacks throughout the day. However, a sweet such as peanut or sesame brittle is sometimes served while a chunk of palm candy with green tea is said to promote digestion. As a special treat, *lephet*, or fermented tea leaf salad, might be served. The main ingredient of this unusual salad is fermented tea leaves; these are then mixed with, or accompanied by, peanuts, roasted sesame seeds, fried garlic, coconut and ginger slices, and so on. Though it may seem unusual to serve a savoury dish after the main meal, this is when *lephet* is often eaten, though you may find it served as a first course in

Opposite:
Buddhist nuns collecting hsoon laung. Each household, rich or poor, gives a portion of its food, usually rice, to monks and nuns.
Left: *An example of the kinds of food that may be offered to monks and nuns in Myanmar.*

Myanmarese restaurants in the West. During monarchical times, much significance was attached to pickled tea leaves, and litigants in a court of law customarily ate pickled tea leaves together after judgment had been handed down, to signify that both parties considered their dispute settled.

After the meal, betel might be chewed, a habit transplanted from neighbouring India that took firm root in Myanmar centuries ago, from the top of society down. In earlier times, tradition called for the paraphernalia associated with the habit to be ceremoniously displayed before the king when he gave a royal audience.

Part Two: Cooking in Myanmar

*No matter how rudimentary the equipment,
the Myanmarese kitchen is the heart and hearth of the home.*

By Win Pe

In the Myanmarese home, the kitchen is sited at the back of the house and serves as an important hub of household activities and communication. It is here that the women of the household discuss family matters, exchange opinions and relate the news and gossip gathered at the market while buying food for the day's meals. All this is done while pounding chilli, crushing onion, deboning fish and filleting meat. The kitchen is the place where family ties are strengthened.

Once made of wood—the basic construction material of a traditional Myanmarese house—the kitchen floor nowadays is more likely to be made of cement. Slippers, usually wooden clogs, are set aside for exclusive wear in the kitchen.

In the village home, the most rudimentary of stoves can be found. Three bricks are positioned to form a triangle on an iron plate; the energy is supplied by sticks of chopped firewood or twigs. The housewife kindles the fire by burning wood shavings or other forms of kindling and blowing on them with a bamboo pipe. In the towns, stoves are more popular, made of a few iron plates and fueled by wood charcoal or sawdust from the local timber mill. Heat is controlled by adding or removing lumps of charcoal with a pair of iron tongs. The electric stove with wire coils between fire-clay plates on an iron stand is common in the suburbs, and gas stoves are now widely used in the cities. Modern kitchens are now being fitted with cooking ranges and for those who can afford them, the microwave oven is a timesaver and a status symbol.

Most kitchens have a meat-safe where the dish cooked for the morning meal is stored, having been made in sufficient quantities to be eaten for the evening meal as well. In addition, the top of the meat-safe serves as a convenient repository for the many condiments necessary for a Myanmarese meal.

In a corner against the wall stand other staples of the local diet: bottles of cooking oil, fish sauce, shrimp sauce, soy sauce and vinegar, as well as pots containing chilli and turmeric powder. Beneath the counter might be found a rice bin, a tin of cooking oil, a smaller tin of sesame oil, a *ngapi* bulge-pot (a glazed pot for storing *ngapi*, or fish paste), a shrimp paste jar, a tamarind fruit crock, a salt jar and a large bottle of dried shrimp.

Opposite: High-tech gadgets are rarely found in rural Myanmar kitchens, but the day's meals are cooked with care and attention. Left: The traditional bamboo strainer can be put to many uses.

Food preparation such as pounding, deboning and filleting are done sitting on a low wooden stool beside the "wet wall". The stove and cooking pots are on the side of the "hot wall". Even in modern kitchens equipped with food-processors, cooks cannot do without the traditional **stone pestle** and **mortar**, nor the **wooden slab** and **wooden rolling pin**. The sound of early morning pounding from the kitchen is a cheerful domestic sound, familiar to all Myanmarese folk.

Most kitchens possess two **woks**: a large, deep wok of cast iron for deep-frying and a smaller, more shallow wok for frying before braising. A **flat pan** is handy for stir-frying and *non-stick pans* are becoming popular to minimise time spent washing-up. **Aluminium pots** with round lids, commonly known by their Indian name of *degchi*, come in a range of sizes and are used for cooking rice, curries and soups. The **rice cooker**, which can be conveniently left alone and produces perfect rice every time, is fast becoming an essential item in the cities where it is common for both husband and wife to work. **Pressure cookers** are occasionally used to save time in busy urban lives, but are not much liked due to a perceived loss in flavour of the dish. However, they are employed to steam *ngathalauk*, a shad-like fish, which needs to be cooked for many hours to soften its multitude of tiny bones. The **earthenware double steamer** found in many kitchens is for steaming banana leaf fish packets or the glutinous rice enjoyed by the northern peoples.

Right: The larger of the two woks found in the Myanmar kitchen is used for deep-frying while a shallow version is reserved for stir-frying.
Far right: Bamboo and wire mesh baskets are useful for fishing out morsels of food from hot oil or water.

In terms of utensils, **wooden ladles** and **wooden spoons** are still preferred. City dwellers, however, are taking advantage of the convenience provided by the **electric blender** and **mixer** to replace the hand-operated whisk or fork. The **wooden spatula** is still employed to stir boiling rice, and to spoon out a few grains so the cook can check whether it has been cooked to the right consistency.

No cook can do without the **perforated spoon**, **colander** and the **wire mesh basket** to retrieve deep-frying items. **Sieves**, according to need, are made of bamboo, metal or cheese-cloth. Four-sided **metal graters** are useful for smaller items but for grating coconut, the traditional grater, *oun gyit*, is best. It comprises a wooden block from which a serrated iron piece protrudes like the prow of a ship. For refined grating, the metal cap of a soft drink bottle is nailed to a short wooden handle and serves as a hand-held grater.

The pride of the kitchen is the wooden chopping block, sliced from the tamarind tree so that the rings show, and the heavy **cleaver** or *dama*. A **Chinese cleaver** is also at hand for lighter jobs. Cutlery is mostly made of ceramic or stainless steel and wooden spoons prove handy but most Myanmars still prefer to eat with their fingers—the food tastes better that way.

Cooking Methods

Myanmar cuisine is not based on complicated techniques,
but there are a few basic methods to master.

By Wendy Hutton

There is a saying in Myanmar—"If not demonstrated by a master, even toasting *ngapi* is unsystematic"—which emphasises the importance of perfecting even the most basic culinary techniques.

The foundation of most "curry style" dishes is a finely ground mixture of onions, garlic, ginger and chillies. In Myanmar, this is achieved by cutting the various items before grinding them with a stone pestle and mortar, but in a Western kitchen, the blender or food processor saves a great deal of time and energy, even if purists complain that the results never taste quite the same.

The onions, garlic and ginger should be peeled and coarsely chopped. If dried chillies are specified, the stem end should be discarded and the chillies torn into two or three pieces before being soaked in warm water for 10–15 minutes to soften. The water should then be drained and discarded. To reduce the heat without losing any of the chilli flavour, discard the seeds which fall into the bottom of the bowl. Put all the ingredients in a blender or food processor and blend to a paste. To keep the blades of the blender turning and achieve a smooth result, add a spoonful or two of the oil specified in the recipe for frying.

If powdered spices such as coriander seeds and cumin are required, a full rich flavour is achieved only by grinding the spices just before usage. Heat the spice seeds gently in a dry pan until they begin to smell fragrant but take great care not to let them colour or this will alter the flavour of the dish. Cool them slightly before grinding to a powder in a clean coffee or spice grinder.

Chilli flakes are as common an accompaniment to Myanmar dishes as salt and pepper to Western food. Rub a heavy pan lightly with oil. Over moderate heat, dry-roast whole dried chillies, stirring frequently, until they are crisp, beginning to change colour and giving off a distinctive fragrance. Let them cool then discard the stem end and grind the chillies coarsely in a clean coffee or spice grinder.

Dried shrimp are ubiquitous, and often used in powdered form. Pick over the shrimp to discard any hardened pieces or bits of shell, then soak them

Dried fish (left) and dried shrimp are just two of the treated fish and shrimp forms (pressed, fermented, salted, etc.) that are a fundamental part of Myanmar cuisine.

Water storage jars from Bagan (Pagan).

lid which covers earthenware cooking pots. This is then put near the fire so that the *ngapi* cooks gently and thoroughly. A more practical method for most cooks is to smooth the *ngapi* over the back of a metal spoon and hold it above a naked flame for several minutes. Alternatively, dry-fry the *ngapi* in a pan over medium heat for several minutes until it becomes dry, crumbly and fragrant.

The first (and perhaps most crucial) stage in cooking a "curry-style" dish is to gently fry the ground ingredients. This must be done using plenty of oil, and cooking over low heat. Don't skimp on the amount of oil specified for this initial frying or the ingredients may burn; if you find the result too oily for your taste, spoon off some of the oil after frying, although a large amount of oil is characteristic of Myanmar cuisine. Myanmar cooks always heat oil in the pan until it is smoking hot, claiming that "cooking" the oil makes it more fragrant. Lower the heat, add the ground ingredients and stir thoroughly for a moment or two. Cover the pan and cook very gently for around 15 minutes, lifting the lid and stirring the contents frequently. When the moisture exuded by the onions has disappeared, remove the lid and keep cooking for a little longer, stirring frequently until "the oil returns" and the contents have turned a reddish-brown with the coloured oil on the surface. Now the dish is ready for the addition of meat, poultry or fish.

in warm water for about 10 minutes. Drain thoroughly and process the dried shrimp in a blender until you get a fine floss. This can be stored in an airtight jar in the refrigerator for many weeks.

Sliced onion and garlic are often deep-fried to a crisp for use as a garnish. Myanmars usually cut the onion in half lengthwise, then slice each half finely crosswise. Garlic should not be too finely sliced. For best results when frying to a crisp, blot the sliced onion and garlic on a paper towels before frying. Heat the oil to moderate and fry (always separately, as garlic cooks more quickly than onion) gently until golden brown. Drain on paper towels and allow to cool completely before bottling. You may like to save time by using packets of deep-fried shallots sold in Asian stores, rather than frying your own onions.

The basic toasting of shrimp paste or *ngapi*, as referred to in the proverb, is done in Myanmar by spreading the paste on the inside of the domed

Myanmarese Ingredients

A guide to the products usually found in the Myanmar pantry.

By Win Pe

BAMBOO SHOOTS: Fresh bamboo shoots must first be peeled, sliced and simmered for 30 minutes till tender. Canned bamboo shoots should be boiled briefly to remove any metallic taste. For the fermented product (*myitchin*), soak the shoots in water for 6 days, changing the water every other day. Mix the shoots thoroughly with salt, compress and place in a large sealed container for three days. Canned fermented bamboo shoots are available from Asian food stores.

BANANA STEM (*nga pyaw oo*): When stripped and sliced, the tender inner part of the lower stem of the banana plant is an essential ingredient in *mohinga*. Banana stem is also added to fish and chicken soups for texture. After slicing, immerse the pieces in water to prevent the stem from turning black. The texture of banana stem is similar to that of celery, crunchy when raw and slightly less so when cooked. The taste is unique but subtle and cannot easily be substituted by any other vegetable—simply omit it from the recipe if it is unavailable.

BASIL: Fresh basil is used frequently in Myanmarese cooking, the *ocimum canum* variety is used as a garnish for bamboo shoot soup and is added to pumpkin curry. Thai basil (*horapa*) is a good substitute; European basil is acceptable.

CHAYOTE: *Sechium edule* is a pear-shaped, squash-like fruit also known as mirliton or christophene. It lends its flavour and succulence to soups, salads and Chinese-style stir-fries, and can be fried in batter to make fritters. Substitute with any mild gourd or squash.

CHILLI (*nga yoke thee*): There are several varieties of chilli commonly used in Myanmar. Tiny red or green bird's-eye chillies, with a taste as sharp as a needle, are finely chopped or left whole and scored to allow their flavour to permeate the dish. The larger, finger-length green chillies and red chillies are sliced and used in both raw and cooked dishes. Dried red chillies are either soaked before being ground to a paste or dried and chopped to make chilli flakes. Dried red chillies are sometimes roasted before grinding to produce roasted chilli powder. Chilli flakes or powder are present on the table at all times.

CINNAMON (*thit jabou*): Cinnamon usually comes in the form of sticks from the bark of the *Cinnamon cassia*, a tree native to Sri Lanka but which is used in butter rice and meat dishes. Avoid using cinnamon powder in recipes where cinnamon sticks are called for.

Boiled (above) and fermented (top) bamboo shoots

Banana stem

Chillies

Cloud ear fungus

Drumstick vegetable

Fermented Horse Gram

Galangal

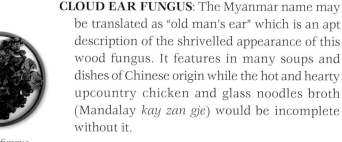

CLOUD EAR FUNGUS: The Myanmar name may be translated as "old man's ear" which is an apt description of the shrivelled appearance of this wood fungus. It features in many soups and dishes of Chinese origin while the hot and hearty upcountry chicken and glass noodles broth (Mandalay *kay zan gje*) would be incomplete without it.

COCONUT MILK: To obtain thick coconut milk, grate, squeeze and strain the flesh of a mature coconut with about ½ cup (125 ml) water. For thin milk, add 2 cups (500 ml) water to the already squeezed mixture. Canned and powdered coconut milk is widely available from Asian food stores.

CORIANDER LEAVES (*nan nan*): Also known as cilantro and Chinese parsley. The fresh leaves are perhaps the most important garnishing item in Myanmar cuisine.

COWPEA (*pelun*): The common cowpea is often used as a filling in savoury dishes. There are usually about 15 pinkish-white to red peas in a pod. Substitute garden peas.

CURRY LEAVES (*pyindawthein*): These small dark green leaves are used as a spice in curries. There are two kinds in Myanmar, the wild and the cultivated. Dried curry leaves are available.

DRUMSTICK VEGETABLE (*dunthalon thee*): *Moringa pterygosperma* is a long, bean-like vegetable with a hard, green skin. The flesh, which must be sucked out when the drumstick is cooked, has a delicate taste and texture. Widely available from Indian food stores.

FERMENTED HORSE GRAM: *Macrotyloma uniflorum*, or horse gram, is cultivated widely in the drier parts of Myanmar, India and Sri Lanka—and on a smaller scale in America and Australia where it is sometimes known as "poor man's gram". The seeds are boiled and fermented in Myanmar to produce an astringent flavouring. No substitutes are available but the ready-made product is sometimes available from Asian food stores, or follow the recipe on page 39.

FERMENTED TEA LEAVES: Tea leaves are steamed until they turn from green to yellow. They are then kneaded until lumps are formed, placed in bamboo baskets, covered with leaves and compressed by a gridwork of split bamboo. The baskets are kept in cellars for 6 months when the leaves are ready to be eaten as *lephet*. Eaten alone, fermented tea leaves are sharp, bitter and pungent yet they marry well with other ingredients to make Fermented Tea Leaf Salad (page 40).

FISH PASTE: Another form of fermented fish integral to Myanmar cuisine. Fish such as anchovies are salted and mashed, then pressed into a pot to ferment for a few days. The odour and taste of fermented fish paste is extremely pungent and it should only be added to recipes in small measures.

FISH SAUCE (*nganpya yay*): This is the liquor which is produced as a by-product of the process of making preserved fish paste. It is used extensively in Myanmar cuisine for its salty flavour; it is often used as a substitute for salt. *Nam pla*, the Thai fish sauce, is a good substitute.

FLOUR: Various kinds of flour are used in Myanmar dishes. **Rice flour** comes in two varieties: ordinary and glutinous. **Wheat flour** is the basis of many "sweets" and is mixed with rice flour to make a crispy batter for fritters. **Chickpea** or *besan* flour is a critical ingredient in many salads and flour made from the soya bean is found in many Shan soups and curries.

GALANGAL: *Alpinia galanga*, a rhizome that resembles ginger in appearance but with a more pinkish hue and a delicate aroma and taste. It is sometimes sold under the Indonesian name, *laos*.

GARAM MASALA: An aromatic blend of spices including cumin, coriander, cinnamon, cardamom, clove, nutmeg and mace that is designed to add flavour and aroma to meat dishes. Ready-made garam masala powder is widely available from Asian food stores.

GARLIC (*kyethun phyu*): Garlic is widely used as a flavouring in all sorts of dishes. It is so often minced and stir-fried for curries that in Myanmar, garlic "chips" can be bought ready-made; these need to be soaked before frying.

GINGER: Is used either fresh and crushed or in dried flakes. Ginger adds flavour to various soups and also forms the chief ingredient in a ginger salad with sesame seeds, peas and oil.

GOURD (*bu*): The gourd is a versatile vegetable that often finds its way to the Myanmarese table. It adds flavour and bulk to curries, and can be fried in batter for a crispy snack. Some of the varieties used are the bottleneck and the opo. Courgette (zucchini) is an adequate substitute.

HORSESHOE LEAVES: The bitter young leaves of the *ipomoea* plant are eaten in salads as well as being used in a variety of medicinal remedies. Substitute with pennywort leaves or daikon cress.

INDIAN MULBERRY: The slightly bitter, edible leaves of the Indian Mulberry tree (*morinda citrifolia*) are used as wrappers for steaming fish. Substitute with Swiss chard.

KAFFIR LIME: Both the leaves and flesh are used in Myanmarese cusine. The leaves impart an intense fragrance to dishes while the flesh is occasionally used in salads. Substitute with limes.

KAILAN: Chinese kale or broccoli often appears in soups of Chinese origin. It also makes a delicious side dish when stir-fried with salt, light soy sauce, garlic and chicken.

LABLAB BEANS: Also known as hyacinth beans, the seeds of *lablab purpureus* are usually sundried in Myanmar and stored for later use. Available from Asian and, sometimes, from North African food stores.

LEEK ROOT (*jumyit*): The root of *allium tuberosumis* is used in sour soups, or chewed whole as an accompaniment to Kneaded Shan Rice (page 46). The rest of the vegetable is occasionally allied with tomato in curries.

LEMONGRASS (*zaba lin*): The stalk adds flavour and aroma to *mohinga*, as well as to other soups and to curries. The leaves are made into a tea which is used as a diuretic. Although available in powder form, it is best used fresh and is widely available in Asian grocery stores.

Bottleneck gourd

Leek root

Kaffir lime

Fermented mustard leaves

Palm sugar

Pennywort

Saw-leaf herb

Sesame seeds

LILY BUDS (*pan chauk*): The Chinese name for dried lily buds translates as "golden needles" which they closely resemble. They are often knotted prior to cooking for a neater appearance. Widely available from Chinese food stores.

LIME (*tham ba ya*): Freshly squeezed lime juice adds a sour tang to salads and is always served in segments with soups such as *mohinga*.

MINT (*pudinan*): Grown widely in Myanmar, this fragrant herb, identical to mint available elsewhere in the world, is used in a variety of soups, salads and other more delicate appetisers.

MUSTARD LEAVES (*mohn-nyin ywet*): The leaves are eaten stir-fried and used in both sweet and sour soups. Mustard leaves are also fermented and served with *meeshay* or rice noodle salad with pork. The leaves are first crushed, dried in the sun, and then marinated for two days in a mixture of salt, ginger, turmeric and rice water. Substitute with Korean *kim chee*.

NOODLES: The **wet rice noodles** for *mohinga* come fermented or unfermented, and in both thin and thick strands. **Dry rice noodles** come in three forms: thick or thin brittle threads, and a less brittle white form, which is used in soups. **Wheat flour noodles** come in round or flat strands, and finally, there are the vermicelli-like transparent glass, or "cellophane", noodles made from mung bean starch.

PALM SUGAR: Made by boiling palmyra palm sap to a treacly consistency and then rolling it into balls when half-cooled. Although it has been replaced by cane sugar in many preparations,

the slightly nutty, smoky flavour of palm sugar is irreplaceable in many preparations. Soft brown sugar may be used as a substitute.

PEAS (*pè*): Myanmar cultivates about twenty varieties of peas and lentils. Among the most widely used are yellow split peas, chickpeas and red beans, all of which are widely available at Asian food stores. Many of the peas are sold in dried form and need to be soaked overnight.

PENNYWORT LEAVES: *Hydrocotyle asiatica* is native to Myanmar. The leaves of this Asian pennywort which are similar in smell and taste to parsley, are found in clear soups, mixed with other ingredients in salads, and eaten raw as a crudité with *ngapi* dip.

RICE: There are two kinds of rice—ordinary and glutinous. The different crops are divided into several classes according to whether the grains are coarse or fine, thick or thin, long or short. Some people prefer the coarser rice because it takes longer to digest, leaving a feeling of fullness longer. Highland folk prefer glutinous rice which is used for sweets in the lowlands. Regular long-grain rice may be used for all recipes except those where glutinous rice is called for.

SAW-LEAF HERB (*Shan nan nan*): The leaves of *eryngium foetidum* have serrated edges, hence the name. The aroma and flavour of saw-leaf herb vaguely resembles coriander leaves (cilantro) which may be substituted for it.

SESAME: Oil from ground sesame seeds is used as a cooking medium and can be drizzled over certain dishes to add flavour. The seeds are often toasted before being used and are sprinkled on snacks and sweets.

SHRIMP PASTE: A pungent smooth paste made from pressed shrimp. It should always be fried or toasted before eating and should be used sparingly. Although there are several versions available in Myanmar, the most widely stocked shrimp pastes in Asian food stores outside the region are Malay *belacan* and Indonesian *trasi*, both of which make perfect substitutes.

SHRIMP, DRIED: Soak in warm water for about 5 minutes to soften and discard any fragments of shell. Dried shrimp are blended to a powdery fluff, or used as they are to flavour soups, salads and condiments.

SORREL (*chin baung*): A plant with very sour leaves, also known as roselle. There are many varieties of sorrel found in Myanmar: common, white, black, red, bitter and wild. Sorrel is often used in sour soups, and is also served fried with bamboo shoots.

SOYA BEAN CAKE (*pè bya*): Dried soya beans are steamed, fermented and made into cakes or wafers, which are roasted and pounded to a powder. This powder is added to curries and soups, or mixed with tomatoes to make a dish similar to Myanmar curried *ngapi*.

SOYA BEAN PRESERVE (*pè ngapi*): Fermented soya beans are made into a paste and used as a condiment. Canned soya bean paste is sold outside Myanmar and can sometimes be used as a substitute for the fermented soya bean products.

SOY SAUCE (*pe nganpya yay*): Light and dark soy sauce both feature in Myanmarese recipes; the light version is saltier and paler in colour.

STAR ANISE (*nanat pwint*): *Illiceum verum* is a dark brown, star-shaped spice with eight hard petals. Star anise has a strong aniseed flavour and is used widely in Chinese cuisine.

STONE PUMPKIN: *Cucurbita pepo* is also known as rock pumpkin or white pumpkin. This vegetable is made into soups, added to curries and mixed with "gold" pumpkin, potato and spices to produce "Indian curry" (*kala hin*).

TAMARIND (*magyi*): Dried tamarind pulp is soaked in water for 10 minutes and squeezed to obtain sour tasting juice. Young tamarind picked early is sometimes called for in recipes but may be substituted with dried tamarind pulp.

TURMERIC (*hsa nwin*): Mostly used in its powder form, this bright yellow rhizome adds both zest and colour to dishes.

WATER SPINACH (*gazun ywet*): Also known as water convolvulus or swamp spinach, this vegetable has arrow-shaped leaves and is excellent stir-fried.

WHITE RADISH (*monlar oo*): A long and large radish frequently called by its Japanese name, *daikon*.

Shrimp paste

Soya bean cake

Stone pumpkin

Water spinach

Part Three: The Recipes

Basic recipes for dips, sauces, pickles and other condiments precede those for main dishes, which begins on page 40.

Fish Sauce Dip

Ngapiyaycho

1 cup (250 ml) water
1 tablespoon preserved fish paste
$1/4$ teaspoon turmeric powder
2 dried red chillies, soaked
2 bird's-eye chillies
1 tablespoon dried shrimp, soaked
2 cloves garlic

Bring the water, fish paste and turmeric powder to a boil, simmer until reduced by half. Strain and discard the solids. Pound the remaining ingredients in a mortar and mix with the fish stock. Serve with raw vegetables.

Tomato Sauce

Khayanchinthee Pantwepyaw

3 tomatoes
2 slices dried fermented soya bean cake,
    7 cm (3 in) in diameter
4 dried red chillies, soaked
3 bird's-eye chillies
2 cloves garlic
1 teaspoon salt
1 tablespoon chopped coriander leaves (cilantro)
1 teaspoon oil

Preheat oven to 200°C (400°F). Bake the tomatoes, dried fermented soya bean cake and dried chillies for 10–15 minutes. Peel the tomatoes. Pound the bird's-eye chillies and garlic in a mortar. Add the soya bean cake slices and salt and continue to pound. Add the tomatoes and the rest of the ingredients. Pound for a further 3–5 minutes. Serve with rice and curries.

Ingredients

When a recipe lists a hard-to-find or unusual ingredient, see pages 31–35 for possible substitutes. If a substitute is not listed, look for the ingredient in your local Asian food market.

Time Estimates

Time estimates for preparation only.

🕐 *quick and very easy to prepare*

🕐🕐 *relatively easy; less than 15 minutes'*
    to prepare

🕐🕐🕐 *takes more than 15 minutes to prepare*

Main Dishes are intended to serve 4

Opposite:
Ngapiyaycho is a potent fish sauce dip which is best served with a selection of raw vegetables.

Green Tamarind Pickle

Mangyitheesein Htaung

2 onions, peeled
1 teaspoon shrimp paste
75 g (1/2 cup) young green tamarind, washed
1/2 teaspoon salt
1 tablespoon dried shrimp, soaked and ground
2 bird's-eye chillies, finely sliced
1 teaspoon chopped *thayetkin* root (*curcuma amada*) (optional)
1 tablespoon oil

Preheat oven to 200°C (400°F). Bake the onions and shrimp paste for 10 minutes and set aside. Scrape the skin off the green tamarind. Grind the green tamarind with the salt in a mortar. Add the onions, shrimp paste and the rest of the ingredients to the mortar and grind to a paste.

Tamarind Sauce

Mangye Chin

2 tablespoons tamarind pulp
1/2 cup (125 ml) warm water
10 g (1/4 cup) chopped mint leaves
2 cloves garlic
3 bird's-eye chillies
1/2 teaspoon salt
1 finger-length red chilli
1/4 teaspoon sugar
1 tablespoon chopped coriander leaves (cilantro)
1 spring onion (green onion), sliced

Soak the tamarind pulp in the water for 20 minutes. Squeeze the pulp by hand, stir and strain to remove any solids. Grind the mint leaves, garlic, bird's-eye chillies, salt, red chilli and sugar in a mortar. Transfer the ground ingredients to the tamarind water, stir and garnish with the coriander leaves and spring onion.

Fried Fermented Soya Bean Cake

Pepoke Gyaw

4 slices dried fermented soya bean cake,
    7 cm (3 in) in diameter
1/2 cup (125 ml) oil, for deep-frying
3 shallots, finely sliced
3 cloves garlic, minced
50 g (1/4 cup) peanuts, coarsely ground
1 tablespoon chilli flakes
3 tablespoons chopped *jumyit* (Indian leek root), sun-dried (optional)

Preheat oven to 200°C (400°F) and bake the fermented soya bean slices for 12–15 minutes. Allow to cool and break into small pieces. Heat the oil in a pan and deep-fry the shallots and garlic separately till crisp. Remove and set aside. Discard the oil, retaining 1 teaspoon in the pan. Add the ground peanuts and fry for 2 minutes. Add the chilli flakes and *jumyit* (if using) and fry for a further 1 minute. Add the soya bean cake slices, shallots and garlic and continue to dry-fry for 1 minute, stirring continuously.

Fried Dried Shrimp with Chilli

Balachaung Gyaw

2/3 cup (175 ml) oil, for deep-frying
3 shallots, sliced
6 cloves garlic, sliced
1 teaspoon shrimp paste
110 g (1 cup) dried shrimp, rinsed and coarsely ground

2 tablespoons fish sauce
2 tablespoons chilli flakes

Heat the oil in a wok and deep-fry the shallots and garlic separately till crisp. Remove with a slotted spoon and set aside. Add the shrimp paste to the oil, stir for a few seconds, then add the ground dried shrimp and fish sauce. Stir-fry over low heat for 8 minutes till the mixture is crisp and fluffy. Add the chilli flakes, continue to stir for 2 minutes till dry and crumbly. Add the crispy shallots and garlic and mix well.

Split-pea Crackers
Pe Chan Gyaw

5 tablespoons rice flour
2 cups (500 ml) water
100 g ($^1/_2$ cup) dried yellow split-peas, soaked
   overnight, drained
$^1/_4$ teaspoon salt
1 cup (250 ml) oil, for deep-frying

Add the rice flour to the water and stir well. Stir in the split-peas and salt. Heat the oil in a wok or deep-fryer till hot. Spoon 1 tablespoon of the mixture into the oil and deep-fry till crisp. Deep-fry several crackers at one time. Drain on paper towels and cool. Crumble by hand if required.

Fermented Horse Gram Sauce
Ponyegyi

500 g (1 lb) horse gram seeds
4 cups (1 litre) water
1 teaspoon salt

Mix all the ingredients in a pan and bring to a boil. Cook for 1 hour then strain the liquid into a earthenware container. Cover with a transparent lid and allow to ferment for 3 days in the sun till a thick black top layer has formed. Stir, then cook for 1 hour over medium heat till the liquid evaporates, stirring continuously. Reduce the heat to low and stir for 10 minutes to allow the paste to thicken. Cool the paste and allow to ferment in a sealed glass jar for a further 3 days in the sun.

Fried Fish Cakes
Ngephe Gyaw

500 g (1 lb) featherback fish (substitute cod,
   kingfish or flounder)
1 clove garlic
1 teaspoon ground ginger
$^1/_4$ teaspoon turmeric powder
$^1/_4$ teaspoon salt
$^1/_2$ teaspoon chilli flakes
Water to moisten fingers
1 cup (250 ml) oil, for deep-frying

Fillet the fish, flake the flesh and transfer to a mortar. Add the garlic and ginger and pound to a paste. Add the turmeric powder, salt and chilli flakes and continue to pound for 10–15 minutes. Roll the mixture into 7-cm long (3-in long) "sausages", moisten your fingers to help shape the mixture. Heat the oil in a pan, add several of the "fish sausages" at one time (not too many as they will expand). Deep-fry for 5 minutes till golden brown. Remove and drain on paper towels.

FERMENTED TEA LEAF SALAD

Lephet Thoke

Lephet is more than just a dish, it is an everyday part of Myanmarese social culture. *Lephet* is served to welcome guests to a house, as a peace offering following an argument, as a snack in front of the television, as a palate cleanser after a meal, even as a stimulant to ward off sleep during all-night Myanmarese opera. And when there is no more food in the house, there will always be some *lephet* in the larder which can be mixed with rice and eaten as is. ①①

    4 tablespoons *lephet* (fermented tea leaves)
    3 cloves garlic, sliced and deep-fried till crisp
    1 bird's-eye chilli, finely chopped
    2 tablespoons dried shrimp, soaked and
       blended to a powdery fluff
    2 tablespoons roasted peanuts
    1 tablespoon toasted sesame seeds
    2 teaspoons lime juice
    2 teaspoons fish sauce
    1 tablespoon oil

Traditionally, *lephet* is served in a lacquer container with different compartments for each ingredient. Diners then choose their ingredients and, using only the thumb and first two fingers of the right hand, delicately serve themselves. Finger bowls would be provided.

Today, most Myanmarese combine all the ingredients in a bowl and mix them thoroughly as with a conventional salad.

Helpful hint: Fermented tea leaves may be available from Indian and Myanmar food stores. Myanmarese ferment young tea leaves by slightly steaming them before packing them into earthenware vessels or bamboo stems and storing them underground for 6 months.

GOURD TEMPURA & SPLIT-PEA FRITTERS

Buthee Gyaw & Paya Gyaw

GOURD TEMPURA

Traditionally, opo gourd is used in this recipe but any gourd or squash, even courgette (zucchini), may be substituted. 🕐

1 cup (250 ml) oil, for deep-frying
300 g (10 oz) gourd (squash)

Batter

7 tablespoons rice flour
2 tablespoons chickpea flour
$^1/_2$ teaspoon baking soda
$^1/_2$ teaspoon salt
$^1/_2$ teaspoon turmeric powder
$^1/_4$ cup (60 ml) water

Prepare the Batter by mixing all the ingredients together in a bowl, making sure the consistency is not too thick. The Batter should run easily off the gourd when coated.

Cut the unpeeled gourd into 10-cm long (4-in long) sticks. Heat the oil in a wok or deep-fryer till hot. Dip 3 sticks of gourd into the Batter and place them gently in the hot oil side by side so that they stick together when deep-fried. Repeat this till about 3–4 clumps are frying in the oil at the same time. Deep-fry for about 8 minutes or till the tempura is golden colour on both sides.

SPLIT-PEA FRITTERS

Served together with Steamed Glutinous Rice with Red Beans (page 48), these fritters make a filling breakfast meal. Alternatively, snack on them throughout the day with lashings of Tamarind Sauce (page 38). 🕐

400 g (2 cups) dried yellow split peas, soaked
    overnight, drained
1 onion, finely sliced
2 bird's-eye chillies, finely chopped
8–10 curry leaves, finely chopped
1 tablespoon finely chopped ginger
$^1/_2$ teaspoon baking soda
1 teaspoon salt
1 cup (250 ml) oil, for deep-frying

Process the peas in a blender in short bursts till a coarse, grainy consistency is achieved. Transfer to a mixing bowl and mix thoroughly by hand with all the other ingredients, except the oil. If the mixture is too dry to form balls, add a few drops of water.

Heat the oil in a wok or pan. Make a ball from 1 heaped tablespoon of the mixture and flatten it slightly. Deep-fry in batches of about 5 balls for 6–7 minutes on each side till both sides are golden brown and crisp. Remove with a slotted spoon and drain on paper towels.

*Opposite:
Gourd Tempura
(left) and Split-pea
Fritters (right).*

BEEF AND MINT SAMOSA & POTATO CUTLETS

Ametha Pudeena Samosa & Aloo Kuttlet

BEEF AND MINT SAMOSA

Delicious eaten with Tamarind Sauce (page 38). 🕐🕐

1¹/₂ teaspoons cumin seeds
1 teaspoon coriander seeds
¹/₂ teaspoon black peppercorns
250 g (8 oz) minced beef
4 cloves garlic, finely chopped
1.25 cm (¹/₂ in) ginger, finely chopped
1¹/₂ tablespoons oil
350 g (2 cups) finely chopped onion
20 g (¹/₂ cup) chopped mint leaves
1¹/₂ teaspoons salt
25–30 spring roll wrappers, cut into 6.5 cm x
    20 cm (2¹/₂ in x 8 in) strips
1 cup (250 ml) oil, for deep-frying

*Opposite:
Beef and Mint
Samosa (left) with
Tamarind Sauce;
and Potato Cutlets
(right).*

Grind the cumin, coriander and peppercorns in a mortar and set aside. Blend the beef with the garlic and ginger. Heat the oil in a pan and stir-fry the beef for 3 minutes over high heat. Add the ground spices and continue to stir-fry for 6 minutes. Add the onion, mint leaves and salt. Fry for a further 2 minutes till dry.

Hold a strip of spring roll wrapper vertically and fold down the top left corner to form a triangular flap at the end. Next, fold down the slanted end to form a rectangle 6.5 cm x 13 cm (2¹/₂ in x 5 in). Fold the top right corner down, turn the wrapper upside down and hold as a cone leaving a 6.5 cm x 6.5 cm (2¹/₂ in x 2¹/₂ in) square flap above it. Insert the meat into the cone and fold down the flap to make a triangle. Seal the wrapper with a dab of water. Heat the oil in a pan and deep-fry till golden brown.

POTATO CUTLETS

Serve with Tamarind Sauce (page 38) or chilli sauce. 🕐🕐

3 cups (750 ml) water
700 g (1¹/₂ lbs) potatoes, peeled and diced
2¹/₂ teaspoons salt
1 tablespoon oil
150 g (5 oz) minced beef
1 teaspoon chilli flakes
3 tablespoons finely sliced onion
3 bird's-eye chillies, finely chopped
1 teaspoon curry powder
Egg white from 1 egg

Boil the water, potato and 1 teaspoon of salt for 15–20 minutes till soft. Drain the water, add 1 teaspoon of salt to the potatoes and mash. Heat the oil in a pan and fry the beef for 3 minutes till brown. Add the chilli flakes, onion, bird's-eye chillies and curry powder, fry for a further 10 minutes. Make the potato patties the size of your palm, place a tablespoon of the beef in the centre and wrap the potato around the beef. Work the stuffed patty till smooth, coat with the egg white and deep-fry till golden brown.

KNEADED SHAN RICE & YELLOW STICKY RICE

Shan Htamin Chin & Kauknyin Sehtamin

KNEADED SHAN RICE

A common past-time at Inle Lake in the Shan highlands is for people to sit at food stalls and eat green packets of rice while chewing on *jumyit*, or Indian leek root. ➋➊

1 cup (250 ml) water
1 whole snakehead fish (about 500 g/1 lb), gutted (substitute flounder or sole)
3 tablespoons fish sauce
2 tomatoes, baked, peeled and deseeded
2 tablespoons oil
5 cloves garlic, sliced
1/2 teaspoon turmeric powder
1 tablespoon chilli flakes
1.2 kgs (6–7 cups) cooked rice
30 pieces 25 cm x 25 cm (10 in x 10 in) banana leaf

Garnishes

100 g (1/2 cup) roasted peanuts
6 bird's-eye chillies, coarsely chopped
25 g (1/2 cup) chopped coriander leaves (cilantro)
3 whole *jumyit* roots (Indian leek roots)

Simmer the water, fish and 2 tablespoons of fish sauce for 15–20 minutes till the water evaporates. Remove the fish and flake the flesh; discard the skin and bones. Grind the tomatoes to a paste. Heat the oil and stir-fry the garlic and turmeric powder for 5 minutes. Switch off the heat and stir-in the chilli flakes. Combine the chilli mixture, cooked rice and fish flesh in a large mixing bowl. Add the remaining fish sauce. Knead for 8–10 minutes till thoroughly combined. Place 85 g (1/2 cup) of the kneaded rice in the centre of a double layer of banana leaves. Wrap the leaves around the rice, secure with a wooden pick. Place in a steamer and steam for 10 minutes. Unwrap the banana leaves (it cannot be eaten) and add the Garnishes (whole or chopped) as desired (chewing on whole bird's-eye chillies can be dangerous).

YELLOW STICKY RICE

Best accompanied by dry roasted beef. ➋➊

675 g (3 cups) uncooked glutinous rice, soaked
4 tablespoons sesame oil
2 tablespoons finely sliced onion
1/2 teaspoon turmeric powder
1 teaspoon salt
2 cups (500 ml) and 2 teaspoons water

Soak the rice for 2 hours and drain. Heat the oil and stir-fry the onion till golden brown, then stir in the turmeric powder. Add the rice, salt and 2 cups (500 ml) of water. Stir, cover and cook over low heat for 35–40 minutes till the rice is done. Sprinkle 2 teaspoons of water over the rice during cooking and stir occasionally.

Opposite: Kneaded Shan Rice, unwrapped and ready to eat (left) and wrapped (above right); and Yellow Sticky Rice (below right).

STEAMED GLUTINOUS RICE WITH RED BEANS & FRIED RICE WITH PEAS

Kauk Nyin Baung & Pe Pyoke Htamin Gyaw

STEAMED GLUTINOUS RICE WITH RED BEANS

This breakfast dish may be eaten alone or with Gourd Tempura (page 42) or Split-pea Fritters (page 39). ☺

> 675 g (3 cups) uncooked glutinous rice, soaked for 1 hour in 3 cups (750 ml) water
> 225 g (1 cup) dried red beans, soaked overnight in 3 cups (750 ml) water
> 4 cups (1 litre) water
> 1 teaspoon salt
> 100 g (1 cup) freshly shredded coconut
> 3¹/₂ tablespoons toasted sesame seeds crushed with 1 teaspoon salt

Opposite:
Steamed Glutinous Rice with Red Beans served with prawns and salted fish (photograph of Fried Rice with Peas appears on page 14).

Drain the water from the glutinous rice. Line a steamer with banana leaves or cheese-cloth. Spread the rice on the leaves or cloth and steam for 1 hour. Meanwhile, drain the red beans and transfer to a saucepan. Add the water and salt, and boil for 30 minutes. Drain and spread the red beans over the steaming rice about 10 minutes before the rice is ready. Continue steaming till the rice is tender. Garnish with the shredded coconut and sesame seeds.

FRIED RICE WITH PEAS

An excellent way of using up yesterday's leftover rice, this dish is normally taken for breakfast in Myanmar. ☺

> 225 g (1 cup) dried whole green peas, or pigeon peas, soaked overnight
> ¹/₂ teaspoon baking soda
> 1 teaspoon salt
> 5 cups (1.25 litres) water
> ¹/₄ cup (60 ml) oil
> 2 tablespoons finely sliced onion
> 1 tablespoon light soy sauce
> 525 g (3 cups) cooked rice
> ¹/₂ teaspoon salt

Drain the peas and transfer to a large pot with the baking soda, salt and water. Bring to a boil, cook for 15 minutes till tender. Drain and set aside. Heat the oil, stir-fry the onion till golden brown. Add the peas and soy sauce, cook for 3–4 minutes. Add the rice and salt, cook and stir gently for a further 5 minutes or till the rice is sufficiently heated.

Helpful hint: Fresh or frozen garden peas may be substituted for dried whole green peas.

PUMPKIN SOUP WITH BASIL

Shwepayon Hincho

The flavours of basil, pepper and pumpkin are blended tantalisingly in this healthful soup. ☻

- **1 tablespoon oil**
- **3 cloves garlic, coarsely chopped**
- **1 pumpkin (about 600 g/1 lb 6 oz) peeled, deseeded and cubed**
- **4 cups (1 litre) chicken stock**
- **Salt and pepper, to taste**
- **1/2 cup (20 g) chopped Thai basil (*horapa*) leaves (substitute European basil)**

Heat the oil in a pan and lightly stir-fry the garlic for 5 minutes till fragrant. Add the pumpkin and chicken stock to the pan and bring to a boil. Cover and simmer for 20 minutes till the pumpkin is tender. Transfer to a blender and process till smooth. Return the soup to the pan and add salt and pepper to taste. Add the chopped basil leaves just before serving.

FISH SOUP WITH DRUMSTICKS & CHICKPEA SOUP WITH CHICKEN

Dunthalon Hinyay & Pekala Chinyay

FISH SOUP WITH DRUMSTICKS ✓

600 g (1 lb 6 oz) snakehead fish steaks
   (substitute red snapper)
2$\frac{1}{2}$ teaspoons salt
4 drumstick vegetables
1 tablespoon tamarind pulp soaked in
   3 tablespoons water
3 tablespoons oil
2 tablespoons minced onion
1 clove garlic, minced
1 teaspoon ground ginger
$\frac{1}{4}$ teaspoon turmeric powder
4 dried red chillies, soaked and ground
1 tomato, diced
3 cups (750 ml) water
15 whole curry leaves

*Opposite:
Fish soup with
Drumsticks (left)
and Chickpea
Soup with Chicken
(right).*

Marinate the fish in 1 teaspoon of salt for 10 minutes. Scrape the skin off the drumstick vegetables, remove the stringy bits and then slice into 5 cm (2 in) thick. Stir and strain the tamarind water, discard the solids. Heat the oil, stir-fry the onion and garlic. Stir in the ginger, turmeric powder and chillies. Add the tomato and cook for 5 minutes; stir continuously and work to a paste. Add the fish and remaining salt, mix well. Cover and cook over medium low heat for 5 minutes. Add the water and bring to a boil, cover and simmer for 5 minutes. Add the drumstick vegetables, tamarind water and curry leaves and simmer for a further 10 minutes.

CHICKPEA SOUP WITH CHICKEN ✓

50 g ($\frac{1}{4}$ cup) chickpeas
4 cups (1 litre) water
1 tablespoon tamarind pulp soaked in
   4 tablespoons water
2 tablespoons oil
2 tablespoons minced onion
1 clove garlic, minced
4 dried red chillies, soaked and ground
2 chicken drumsticks, skinned and cut into
   3 pieces each
150 g (5 oz) dried salted fish, cut into
   2.5-cm (1-in) strips, soaked
2 tablespoons fish sauce
100 g (4 oz) bottleneck gourd, cubed
1 Asian eggplant, cubed
1 tomato, cut into 8 wedges
1 teaspoon salt
8–10 whole curry leaves
1 teaspoon garam masala

Boil the chickpeas in 2 cups (500 ml) of water for 30 minutes till soft. Strain the tamarind water, discard the solids. Heat the oil, stir-fry the onion, garlic and chilli paste. Add the chicken and salted fish, cover and cook for 5 minutes. Add the remaining water and fish sauce, cover and boil for 5 minutes. Add the chickpeas, together with the water, and the rest of the ingredients. Simmer for a further 10 minutes.

MUSHROOM SOUP WITH WATER SPINACH

Mho Hingyo

A simple and healthful broth which may be served as a side dish during any meal. ①

1 tomato, cut into wedges
1 teaspoon salt
2 cups (500 ml) chicken stock
200 g (7 oz) button or straw mushrooms, quartered
30 g (1 cup) water spinach
Ground black pepper, to taste

Place the tomato, salt and chicken stock in a pan, bring to a boil and simmer for 5 minutes. Add the mushrooms and continue to simmer for 10 minutes. Add the water spinach 2 minutes before the end of cooking. Add the ground black pepper to taste.

Helpful hint: Prepare homemade chicken stock by simmering chicken bones in water over low heat for a minimum of 1 hour (stock can be frozen for later use).

FERMENTED BAMBOO SHOOT SOUP & STONE PUMPKIN SOUP WITH CHICKEN

Myitchin Hinyay & Kyaukpayon Hingcho

FERMENTED BAMBOO SHOOT SOUP

Fermented bamboo shoots impart a unique flavour to any dish and combine well with the meat and spices in this slow-cooked soup. ⊘⊘

2 tablespoons oil
3 tablespoons ground onion
1 clove garlic, ground
4 dried red chillies, soaked and ground
1 teaspoon ground ginger
400 g (14 oz) pork loin, cubed
300 g (10 oz) fermented bamboo shoots
6 cups (1.5 litres) water
1 teaspoon salt

Opposite:
Stone Pumpkin
Soup with
Chicken (left)
and Fermented
Bamboo Shoot
Soup (right).

Heat the oil over medium-high heat and stir-fry the onion, garlic, chillies and ginger till fragrant. Add the meat and stir-fry for 3–5 minutes. Add the fermented bamboo shoots, water and salt. Bring to a boil, reduce the heat to low and slow-cook for 2 hours.

Helpful hint: If using canned fermented bamboo shoots, drain any excess liquid before cooking. To make fermented bamboo shoots at home, marinate fresh bamboo shoots in salt in a sealed container for 3 days.

STONE PUMPKIN SOUP WITH CHICKEN

A simple broth that may be served as a side dish for lunch or dinner. ⊘

3 cups (750 ml) water
2 tablespoons fish sauce
3 cloves garlic, minced
300 g (1 cup) cubed boneless chicken breast
200 g (1 cup) cubed and deseeded pumpkin
$1/2$ teaspoon ground white pepper

Bring the water, fish sauce and garlic to a boil. Add the chicken and simmer for 6 minutes. Add the pumpkin and continue to simmer for 6 minutes. Stir in the pepper just before the end of cooking.

VERMICELLI SOUP WITH CLOUD EAR FUNGUS

Kyasan Chet

A wonderfully fragrant chicken soup with a real chilli and pepper kick. Popular among all Myanmarese, this dish is often served on ceremonial occasions. ⓙⓙⓙ

2 tablespoons oil
2 tablespoons ground onion
4 dried red chillies, soaked and ground
3 cloves garlic, ground
200 g (7 oz) boneless chicken, cubed
6 cups (1.5 litres) chicken stock
150 g (5 oz) transparent vermicelli, soaked in hot water
15 g (½ cup) dried cloud ear fungus, soaked in hot water (yields 150 g/2 cups, when drained)
1 sheet dried soya bean, approximately 15 cm x 20 cm (6 in x 8 in), soaked in hot water
6 tablespoons fish sauce
1 tablespoon ground black pepper
30 g (1 oz) dried lily buds (optional)

Garnishes
25 g (½ cup) chopped coriander leaves (cilantro)
2 limes, quartered

Heat the oil over medium-high heat and stir-fry the ground onion, chillies and garlic till fragrant. Add the chicken and stir-fry for 5 minutes till the chicken is half-cooked. Add the chicken stock and bring to a boil.

Drain the vermicelli, cloud ear fungus and soya bean sheet. With a pair of kitchen scissors, cut each into bite-size pieces and add to the soup. Stir in the fish sauce and pepper. Add the dried lily buds (if using). Boil for 15 minutes. Garnish with the coriander leaves and lime wedges.

Helpful hints: Hard-boiled quail eggs may be added to the soup as well as slices of Fried Fish Cakes (page 39).

COCONUT NOODLES

Ohn-no Kyaukswe

A perennial favourite in Myanmar, this fantastic soupy noodle dish is flavoured with coconut and chicken. Although rather slow to prepare, it is ideal for parties. Simply place each food item in a separate dish on the table and let guests choose their own garnishes. ☺☺☺

500 g (1 lb) boneless chicken, cubed
6 tablespoons fish sauce
¼ cup (60 ml) oil
3 tablespoons ground onion
1 tablespoon ground garlic
½ tablespoon ground ginger
½ teaspoon turmeric powder
1 tablespoon chilli flakes
50 g (½ cup) chickpea flour
1 cup (250 ml) water
7 cups (1.75 litres) chicken stock
1⅓ cups (330 ml) coconut milk
2 kgs (4 lbs) fresh egg noodles, blanched in
    boiling water

Garnishes
4 hard-boiled eggs, peeled and sliced
1 onion, soaked and finely sliced
25 g (½ cup) chopped coriander leaves
    (cilantro)
2 limes, quartered
350 g (12 oz) fresh egg noodles, deep-fried
    in 1 cup (250 ml) oil till crisp, drained on
    paper towels, cooled and crumbled by hand
    into bite-size pieces

7 tablespoons chilli flakes
Fish sauce

Marinate the chicken with the fish sauce for at least 15 minutes. Heat the oil in a large pan, stir-fry the onion, garlic, ginger and turmeric powder for 5 minutes. Stir in the chicken and chilli flakes. Cover and cook over medium-low heat for 10 minutes. Stir occasionally to prevent the chicken from sticking to the pan. Meanwhile, add the chickpea flour to the water and whisk to remove any lumps.

Add the chicken stock to the pan and bring to a boil. Reduce the heat, add the chickpea flour paste, cover and simmer for a further 10 minutes. Add the coconut milk and continue to simmer for 30–40 minutes, stirring occasionally, till the sauce thickens slightly.

Arrange each Garnishes ingredients on a separate plate on the table around a central bowl of chicken and coconut soup.

To serve, take a portion of the blanched fresh egg noodles, add a little of each Garnishes (a dash of fish sauce if desired) and a generous helping of the chicken and coconut soup.

RICE NOODLE FISH SOUP

Mohinga

Mohinga is virtually the national dish of Myanmar and there are many regional variations. ☉☉☉

300 g (10 oz) rice vermicelli noodles, soaked for 2 minutes and boiled for 2¹/₂ minutes, drained and tossed with a little oil

Stock

- **1 kg (2 lbs) whole catfish**
- **5 stalks lemongrass, tender inner part of bottom third only, bruised**
- **1 teaspoon turmeric powder**
- **4 tablespoons fish sauce**
- **8 cups (2 litres) water**

Soup

- **150 g (³/₄ cup) uncooked rice, dry-roasted till light brown and ground to a powder**
- **12 cups (3 litres) water**
- **4 dried red chillies**
- **100 g (1 cup) coarsely chopped onion**
- **3 cloves garlic, minced**
- **1 teaspoon ground ginger**
- **2 tablespoons coarsely ground lemongrass, tender inner part of bottom third only**
- **¹/₂ cup (125 ml) oil**
- **¹/₂ teaspoon turmeric powder**
- **1¹/₂ teaspoons salt**
- **1 teaspoon ground black pepper**
- **3 tablespoons fish sauce**
- **12 whole shallots, peeled**
- **200 g (7 oz) banana stem, sliced 1 in (2.5 cm) thick (optional)**

Garnishes

- **4 hard-boiled eggs, peeled and quartered**
- **1 onion, finely sliced and fried with a pinch of turmeric till crisp**
- **Split-pea Crackers (page 39), crumbled**
- **Fried Fish Cakes (page 39)**
- **3 spring onions (green onions), sliced**
- **25 g (¹/₂ cup) chopped coriander leaves (cilantro)**
- **4 limes, quartered**
- **Fish sauce**
- **Chilli flakes**

Prepare the Stock by placing all the ingredients in a large pan and bring to a boil. Reduce the heat, cover and cook for 20 minutes. Remove the fish, flake the flesh and set aside. Strain the Stock and discard the solids.

Prepare the Soup by adding the rice powder to the water, stir and set aside. Blend the chillies, onion, garlic, ginger and lemongrass to a paste. Heat the oil in a pan and stir-fry the chilli paste with the turmeric powder till fragrant. Stir in the fish, then add the salt, pepper, fish sauce and whole shallots and continue to cook for 5 minutes. Add the banana stem, reserved Stock and rice powder water. Bring to a boil, stirring to prevent any lumps forming. Boil for 15 minutes, reduce the heat and simmer for a further 20 minutes.

To serve, place a portion of the noodles into a bowl, add a little of each of the Garnishes, then add a generous helping of the Soup.

CRISPY FRIED NOODLE SOUP & BOTTLENECK GOURD SOUP

Kyaukswe Kywt Hincho & Buthee Hingha

CRISPY FRIED NOODLE SOUP

"Hincho" denotes a mild broth and in this dish, either chicken or duck broth can be used. Here the *hincho* is sweetened by pepper and garlic. ⏱

150 g (5 oz) dried thin egg noodles or 350 g (12 oz) fresh egg noodles
1 cup (250 ml) oil, for deep-frying
6 cups (1.5 litres) chicken stock
125 g (1 cup) cubed boneless chicken
3 cloves garlic, crushed
1/2 tablespoon salt
225 g (1 cup) green peas (optional)
1/2 teaspoon ground white pepper
3 spring onions (green onions), sliced
25 g (1/2 cup) chopped coriander leaves (cilantro)

If using dried noodles, boil in water till just soft, then drain and cool. Deep-fry the noodles a handful at a time till crispy (spread the noodles around the pan to create a lattice-work effect). Set aside.

Bring the chicken stock to a boil. Add the chicken and garlic, cover and simmer for 5 minutes. Add the salt and green peas (if using) and simmer for a further 5 minutes. Stir in the pepper.

To serve, place 1/4 cup deep-fried noodles in a bowl and add the chicken soup. Garnish with spring onions and coriander leaves.

BOTTLENECK GOURD SOUP

The term "hingha" indicates a peppered soup and is considered a universal cure-all. Substitute 1 tablespoon dried shrimp, rinsed and ground, for the smoked dried catfish which is difficult to find outside Myanmar. ⏱

1 smoked dried catfish (substitute 1 tablespoon dried shrimp, soaked, rinsed and ground)
2 cups (500 ml) water for the catfish
100 g (1 cup) peeled, deseeded and cubed bottleneck gourd
3 cloves garlic, minced
1 teaspoon ground black pepper
2 1/2 cups (625 ml) water
1 teaspoon salt

If using smoked dried catfish, boil the fish in 2 cups (500 ml) of water for 5 minutes. Remove the fish and flake the flesh; discard the bones and water. If catfish is unavailable, rinse and grind 1 tablespoon dried shrimp.

Place the fish flakes (or ground dried shrimp), gourd, garlic, pepper, water and salt into a saucepan. Boil over high heat for 5 minutes. Reduce the heat to medium-low and simmer for 10 minutes.

Opposite: Crispy Fried Noodle Soup (left) and Bottleneck Gourd Soup (right).

ARAKAN RICE NOODLES IN FISH SOUP

Rakhine Monti

The state of Rakhine, formerly known as Arakan, is located on the west coast of Myanmar, facing the Bay of Bengal. The Arakan people are excellent fishermen and catch a wide variety of seafood. Traditionally, this recipe uses meat from the fleshy conger eel but grouper may be substituted. ◑◑◓

6 cups (1.5 litres) water
250 g ($^{1}/_{2}$ lb) conger eel (substitute grouper), skinned
1 teaspoon salt
1 tablespoon fish sauce
3 cloves garlic, crushed
1 tablespoon shrimp paste
5 cm (2 in) galangal or ginger, bruised
1 teaspoon ground black pepper
300 g (10 oz) rice vermicelli noodles, soaked for 2 minutes and boiled for $2^{1}/_{2}$ minutes
2 tablespoons tamarind pulp soaked in $^{1}/_{2}$ cup (125 ml) water, stir and strained, discard the solids
12 cloves garlic, sliced and deep-fried with $^{1}/_{4}$ teaspoon turmeric powder
6 bird's-eye chillies, ground
25 g ($^{1}/_{2}$ cup) chopped coriander leaves (cilantro)
Split-pea Crackers (page 39), crumbled by hand

Bring $3^{1}/_{4}$ cups (800 ml) of the water, the fish, salt and fish sauce to a boil and simmer for 15 minutes. Remove the fish from the stock and, when cool, flake the flesh and discard the bones. Transfer the fish stock to a blender, add the garlic and boneless fish meat, blend for 30–40 seconds.

Boil the shrimp paste in the remaining water for 10 minutes. Add the blended fish stock and galangal or ginger. Simmer for 20 minutes. Add the ground black pepper and stir.

To serve, place a portion of the rice vermicelli noodles into a bowl, add 1 tablespoon of the tamarind water, 1 teaspoon fried garlic, a sprinkling of ground bird's-eye chillies, coriander leaves and Split-pea Crackers. Top with a generous portion of the fish and fish soup.

RICE NOODLE SALAD WITH PORK

Mandalay Meeshay

A specialty of Mandalay, this dish combines pork curry with noodles and an assortment of garnishes. Best served with a peppery chicken soup. ①①①

1/4 cup (60 ml) oil
1 star anise
4 tablespoons sliced onion
3 cloves garlic, sliced
500 g (1 lb) lean pork, diced
1 tomato, diced
1 teaspoon salt
1/2 cup (125 ml) water

Garnishes

75 g (1/2 cup) cornflour
2 cups (500 ml) water
80 g (1 cup) beansprouts
250 g (8 oz) medium-thick rice noodles
4 tablespoons preserved sweet soya beans
4 teaspoons light soy sauce
4 tablespoons chopped fermented mustard
   leaves (substitute Korean *kim chee*)
4 tablespoons ground roasted peanuts
25 g (1/2 cup) chopped coriander leaves
   (cilantro)
3 tablespoons chilli flakes
Fish sauce

Heat the oil in a pan and stir-fry the star anise for 2 minutes. Remove the star anise and grind. Add the onion and garlic to the oil and stir-fry for 5 minutes till fragrant. Add the pork, ground star anise, tomato and salt. Stir-fry for 5 minutes then add the water, cover and cook over medium-low heat for 8–10 minutes, stirring occasionally.

Prepare the Garnishes by heating the cornflour and water and stir continuously till the mixture becomes a translucent jelly. Boil the beansprouts for 2 minutes. Soak the noodles for 2 minutes then boil till soft.

To serve, place a portion of the noodles in each bowl. Add 2 tablespoons of the pork curry, 1 tablespoon beansprouts, 1 tablespoon cornflour mixture, 1 teaspoon preserved soya beans, 1/2 teaspoon soy sauce, 1/2 tablespoon fermented mustard leaves and 1/2 teaspoon peanuts. Sprinkle the coriander leaves, chilli flakes and fish sauce over the salad. Mix well.

HORSESHOE LEAF SALAD

Myin Khwa Ywet Thoke

This light and crunchy salad successfully marries the bitterness of the horseshoe leaves with the sweetness of the peanuts and sesame seeds. In Myanmar, the leaves are considered to have medicinal properties and are believed to be especially good for the kidneys. ⊘

1/4 cup (60 ml) oil, for deep-frying
12 cloves garlic, sliced
30 g (1/4 cup) dried shrimp, soaked
4 tablespoons finely sliced onion, soaked
100 g (2 cups) horseshoe leaves (substitute any green leaves such as pennywort leaves or daikon cress), washed
2 teaspoons fish sauce
2 teaspoons ground, roasted peanuts
1 tablespoon toasted sesame seeds
2 bird's-eye chillies, finely sliced
1 teaspoon lime juice

Heat the oil and deep-fry the garlic till crisp. Remove the garlic and retain the oil. Drain the dried shrimp and blend to a powdery fluff. Drain the onion slices. Combine all the ingredients, including 1 teaspoon of the garlic-infused oil, on a large plate and toss well.

DAIKON SALAD & GRILLED EGGPLANT SALAD

Monlar Oo Thoke & Khayanthee Thoke

DAIKON SALAD

This refreshing salad can be eaten as a starter or as an accompaniment to curries and rice. ◑◷

- 3 tablespoons rice vinegar
- 1 teaspoon salt
- 1 tablespoon sugar
- 1 daikon radish (about 500 g/1 lb), peeled and finely sliced
- 9 cloves garlic, finely chopped
- 3 tablespoons oil
- 2 tablespoons peanuts
- 1 onion, sliced, soaked in cold water for 5 minutes, drained
- 1 tablespoon toasted sesame seeds
- 1 teaspoon fish sauce
- 2 tablespoons chopped coriander leaves (cilantro)

*Opposite:
Daikon Salad
(left) and Grilled
Eggplant Salad
(right).*

Mix the rice vinegar, salt and sugar in a salad bowl and whisk till the salt and sugar are dissolved. Add the radish, toss and chill for 15 minutes. Fry the chopped garlic in the oil over high heat till golden, remove with a slotted spoon and drain on paper towels. Dry-roast the peanuts in a pan, cool and grind finely. When ready to serve, remove the radish mixture from the refrigerator and drain any excess liquid. Add the remaining ingredients and toss well.

GRILLED EGGPLANT SALAD

A delightful salad that surprises with each bite. The smoky flavours of grilled eggplant blend with piquant chilli and crunchy, sweet sesame. ◑◷

- 2 Asian eggplants
- 2 tablespoons oil
- 6 cloves garlic, sliced
- 2 tablespoons finely sliced onion, soaked in water, then drained
- 2 tablespoons chopped roasted peanuts
- 1 tablespoon toasted sesame seeds
- 2 bird's-eye chillies, finely sliced
- 2 teaspoons fish sauce
- 2 tablespoons chopped coriander leaves (cilantro)

Grill the eggplants over charcoal flame till the skin is lightly charred; alternatively, bake or cook under grill (broil) till soft. Cool, discard the skin and mash the flesh.

Heat the oil in a wok, add the garlic and deep-fry till crisp. Remove with a slotted spoon and retain the oil.

Place the eggplants, onion, garlic, peanuts, sesame seeds, chillies and fish sauce in a salad bowl. Add 1 teaspoon of the garlic-infused oil and mix well. Garnish with the coriander leaves.

TOSSED NOODLE SALAD

Let Thoke Sone

A healthful assortment of vegetables, noodles and tofu which diners select and mix by hand. Let Thoke Sone can be found in roadside stalls throughout Myanmar and is traditionally eaten with Bottleneck Gourd Soup (page 64). ②②②

4 potatoes, peeled and cubed
2 cakes (firm) beancurd cakes (about 300 g/10 oz), soaked
1/4 cup (60 ml) oil, for deep-frying
1 finger-length red chilli, finely chopped
85 g (1/2 cup) cooked rice
200 g (7 oz) fresh egg noodles, blanched
90 g (3 oz) transparent vermicelli, soaked 2 minutes and boiled for 3 minutes
50 g (1 cup) shredded cabbage
80 g (1 cup) beansprouts, blanched
150 g (1 cup) shredded green papaya
1 tomato, peeled and chopped
160 g (1 cup) peeled and shredded cucumber

Garnishes

2 tablespoons oil
1 onion, finely sliced
12 cloves garlic, finely sliced
2 tablespoons chilli flakes
2 tablespoons tamarind pulp soaked in 1/2 cup (125 ml) water
3 bird's-eye chillies, finely sliced
1 teaspoon sugar syrup
4 tablespoons dried shrimp, soaked and blended to a powdery fluff
4 tablespoons roasted pea flour
4 tablespoons fish sauce
25 g (1/2 cup) chopped coriander leaves (cilantro)

Boil the potatoes till done. Drain the beancurd cakes and pat dry with paper towels. Slice each one in half then cut each half into 9 pieces to yield 36 cubes. Heat the oil, add the beancurd and deep-fry over medium-high heat for 5 minutes till golden on all sides. Remove with a slotted spoon and set aside. Knead the chilli into the cooked rice to color it.

Prepare the Garnishes by heating the oil in a pan and stir-fry the onion and garlic till crisp. Remove and set aside, retain the oil. Stir-fry the chilli flakes by spooning the retained hot oil onto the chilli flakes in a separate bowl and set aside (if chilli flakes are placed directly into very hot oil, they will burn immediately). Stir and strain the tamarind water, discard the solids. Add the bird's-eye chillies and sugar syrup to the tamarind water and set aside.

To serve, arrange all the main ingredients on a large plate. Place each of the Garnishes in individual bowls. Take a small handful of each item from the main ingredients. Then sprinkle on a little of each of the Garnishes and mix thoroughly by hand.

GREEN MANGO SALAD & GREEN PAPAYA SALAD

Thayetthee Thoke & Thinnbawthee Thoke

GREEN MANGO SALAD

This light and refreshing salad is fast to prepare and can be eaten alone as a snack on a hot day or with other dishes as part of a meal. ☉

- 300 g (2 cups) peeled and shredded green mango
- 1 teaspoon shrimp paste
- 30 g (¼ cup) dried shrimp, soaked and blended to a powdery fluff
- 4 tablespoons finely sliced onion, soaked
- 6 cloves garlic, finely sliced
- 2 tablespoons oil
- 2 teaspoons fish sauce
- 1 tablespoon coarsely ground, roasted peanuts
- 1 tablespoon toasted sesame seeds
- 2 bird's-eye chillies, finely sliced

Soak the mango in water for 10 minutes, then drain and squeeze out any excess water. Dry-roast the shrimp paste in a wok over low heat for 3 minutes. Combine all the ingredients in a bowl and mix well.

GREEN PAPAYA SALAD

Look for a slightly unripe papaya which adds a hint of sourness to the salad. ☉

- 2 tablespoons oil
- 6 cloves garlic, finely sliced
- 1 teaspoon chilli flakes
- 1 teaspoon tamarind pulp soaked in 1 tablespoon water
- 300 g (2 cups) peeled, deseeded and shredded green papaya
- 4 tablespoons finely sliced onion, soaked
- 2 teaspoons fish sauce
- 2 bird's-eye chillies, finely sliced
- 30 g (¼ cup) dried shrimp, soaked and blended to a powdery fluff
- 1 tablespoon roasted pea flour

Heat the oil in a pan and deep-fry the garlic till crisp. Remove and set aside, retaining the oil. Stir-fry the chilli flakes by spooning the retained hot oil onto the chilli flakes in a bowl and set aside. Stir and strain the tamarind water, discard the solids. Place all the ingredients, including the chilli oil, in a bowl and mix thoroughly.

*Opposite:
Green Mango
Salad (left) and
Green Papaya
Salad (right).*

KAFFIR LIME SALAD

Shauthee Thoke

The sharp flavour of this citrus salad will make your cheeks pucker and salivary glands go into overdrive. Myanmarese avoid this by eating the salad with a hot peppery soup. ⏱

1 teaspoon shrimp paste
2 tablespoons dried shrimp, soaked
1 onion, finely sliced and soaked
100 g (½ cup) chopped kaffir lime flesh
   (substitute small limes or grapefruit)
1 tablespoon chilli flakes
1 bird's-eye chilli, finely sliced
2 tablespoons garlic oil

Dry-roast the shrimp paste in a wok over low heat for 5 minutes. Drain the dried shrimp and blend to a powdery fluff. Drain the onion slices. Mix all the ingredients together in a salad bowl.

Helpful hints: If kaffir limes are unavailable, grapefruit or the flesh of small limes may be used as a substitute. Although the flavour is less aromatic than kaffir limes, it may be enhanced by the addition of thinly sliced kaffir lime leaves which tend to be more readily available than the fruit. Frozen kaffir lime leaves are perfectly acceptable.

Make your own garlic oil by frying sliced garlic in oil till crisp. Remove the garlic with a slotted spoon and retain for other recipes. Garlic oil is also available from Asian food stores.

FRIED FISH CAKE SALAD

Ngephe Thoke

Commercially available fish cakes pale in comparison to the delicious homemade ones used in this salad recipe. An excellent all-purpose salad that is tasty and filling enough to be eaten on its own as well as with other main dishes. ☺☺☺

1 portion Fried Fish Cakes (page 39)
3 tablespoons oil
6 cloves garlic, coarsely chopped
1 onion, sliced and soaked
3 tablespoons oil
1 bird's-eye chilli, finely chopped
3–4 kaffir lime leaves, finely chopped
12 g (¼ cup) chopped coriander leaves (cilantro)
1 teaspoon kaffir lime juice (substitute juice of small limes)

Opposite:
Fried Fish Cake
Salad with cooked
coconut milk
sauce.

Prepare the Fried Fish Cakes by following the recipe on page 39. Cut each fish cake into diagonal slices.

Heat the oil and deep-fry the garlic till crisp. Remove with a slotted spoon and set aside. Retain the oil. Drain the onion slices. To assemble the salad, place the fish cake slices in a bowl and mix thoroughly with all the ingredients including a teaspoon of the garlic-infused oil.

Helpful hint: This salad is often served with a dollop of cooked coconut milk sauce (as shown in photo). To make the sauce, bring about ½ cup (125 ml) coconut milk to a boil and simmer gently, stiring continuously, for about 5 minutes or till the liquid reduces to about 1 tablespoon.

SLOW-COOKED HILSA FISH & CATFISH IN TAMARIND SAUCE

Ngathalaukbaung & Ngakhu Chet

SLOW-COOKED HILSA FISH

An extraordinary recipe which melts all the bones, including the centre bone, of the hilsa or shad, while leaving the flesh firm and full of flavour. 🕐🕐

Opposite:
Slow-cooked Hilsa
Fish (above)
and Catfish
in Tamarind
Sauce (below).
The catfish may
be sliced, see
photograph, or left
whole, see recipe.

500 g (1 lb) whole shad or herring, head removed, gutted and cut in two
2 tablespoons white vinegar
1 tablespoon fish sauce
1½ teaspoons salt
½ teaspoon ginger, ground
¼ teaspoon turmeric powder
¼ cup (60 ml) oil
2 tablespoons ground onion
1 clove garlic, ground
2 dried red chillies, soaked and ground
1 teaspoon sugar
1 teaspoon chilli flakes
1 tomato, cut into wedges
4 stalks lemongrass, tender inner part of bottom third only, bruised
7 cm (3 in) coriander root (optional)
1½ cups (375 ml) water

Score the fish and marinate in the vinegar, fish sauce, salt, ginger and turmeric powder for 30 minutes. Heat the oil and stir-fry the onion, garlic and chilli paste till fragrant. Stir in the sugar and chilli flakes, then add the tomato and fish. Cook over medium heat for 5 minutes. Place the lemongrass and coriander root (if using) in a pressure cooker and cover with the fish and gravy. Add the water and simmer over medium-low heat for 3–3½ hours.

CATFISH IN TAMARIND SAUCE

The sweetness in the sauce perfectly balances the tamarind in this appetizing dry catfish curry. 🕐🕐

4 catfish, about 500 g (1 lb) (substitute red snapper), gutted and heads removed
½ teaspoon salt
1 cup (250 ml) water
2 tablespoons fish sauce
2 tablespoons tamarind pulp soaked in ½ cup (125 ml) water
3 tablespoons oil
2 tablespoons minced onion
1 clove garlic, ground
1 tablespoon sugar
1 teaspoon chilli flakes
25 g (½ cup) chopped coriander leaves (cilantro)

Score the fish diagonally and marinate in the salt for 10 minutes. Transfer the fish to a pan, add the water and fish sauce, cover and simmer for 6–8 minutes. Squeeze the tamarind pulp, stir, strain and discard the solids. Heat the oil in a separate pan and stir-fry the onion and garlic till fragrant. Stir in the sugar and chilli flakes. Add the fish and mix well. Add the tamarind water, cover and cook for 10 minutes. Garnish with the coriander leaves.

SNAKEHEAD FISH IN MULBERRY LEAF PACKETS

Ngayan Yeyoywet

The slightly bitter leaves of the Indian Mulberry tree (*morinda citrifolia*) are stuffed with fragrant fish and steamed. The Indian Mulberry tree is widely sought after for its fruit, commonly known as *noni*, which is believed to possess numerous medicinal qualities. 🕐🕐

> **500 g (1 lb) snakehead fish fillets (substitute catfish or snapper)**
> **2 teaspoons salt**
> **2 tablespoons roasted rice flour**
> **$1/2$ cup (125 ml) water**
> **3 tablespoons oil**
> **2 tablespoons minced onion**
> **1 clove garlic, minced**
> **$1/2$ teaspoon chopped ginger**
> **1 teaspoon chilli flakes**
> **30 Indian Mulberry leaves (substitute Swiss chard leaves)**

Marinate the fillets with the salt for 15 minutes then flake the flesh. Soak the roasted rice flour in the water. Heat the oil in a pan and stir-fry the onion and garlic till fragrant. Stir in the ginger and chilli flakes. Add the fish and stir-fry for 2–3 minutes. Add the rice flour paste and mix well. Do not cover, cook for a further 5 minutes, stirring occasionally.

Arrange the two leaves side by side slightly overlapping. Place 3–4 tablespoons, or more, of the fish mixture in the centre of the leaves and, if necessary, add one more leaf underneath and perpendicular to the first two. Wrap the leaves around the fish mixture and fasten at the top with kitchen string or a wooden pick, or both. Place in a steamer and steam for 10 minutes.

PRAWNS IN TOMATO CURRY

Pazunhtok Sebyan

For this spicy curry, use the freshest available tiger prawns or other large prawns. Serve with plain rice and stir-fried vegetables. ⓙⓙ

500 g (1 lb) tiger prawns, shelled and cleaned
1 tablespoon fish sauce
1/3 cup (80 ml) oil
2 tablespoons minced onion
3 cloves garlic, minced
1/4 teaspoon turmeric powder
1 tablespoon chilli flakes
2 tomatoes, cut in wedges
1 finger-length green chilli, halved lengthwise
1/2 teaspoon salt
2 tablespoons chopped coriander leaves
    (cilantro)

Marinate the prawns in the fish sauce for at least 15 minutes. Heat the oil in a pan and stir-fry the onion and garlic for 5 minutes till fragrant. Stir in the turmeric powder. Lower the heat and add the chilli flakes, tomatoes, green chilli and salt. Cook for 6–8 minutes, stirring to form a paste. Add the prawns and coriander leaves and cook for 3–4 minutes, stirring frequently, till the prawns are done.

MYANMARESE CRAB CURRY

Ganan Hin

The natural sweetness of the crab and onion is complemented by the sour tang of tamarind and the fragrant aroma of garam masala. 🕐🕑

4 cups (1 litre) water
4 whole live crabs, about 1 kg (2 lbs)
4 dried red chillies, soaked
3 tablespoons chopped onion
2 whole cloves garlic
2 tablespoons oil
¼ teaspoon turmeric powder
1 tablespoon fish sauce
2 teaspoons tamarind pulp soaked in
    2 tablespoons water
1 teaspoon garam masala
1 cup (250 ml) water

Bring 4 cups (1 litre) water to a boil. Plunge the live crabs into the boiling water for 3 minutes and drain. Clean the crabs and discard the spongy grey matter. Use a cleaver to chop the crab into large pieces; smash the claws lightly with the side of a cleaver to allow the flavours to penetrate.

Drain the chillies and transfer to a blender, add the onion and garlic and blend to a paste. Heat the oil in a pan, stir-fry the chilli paste for 4 minutes till fragrant. Stir in the turmeric powder and fry for a further 1 minute. Add the crab and fish sauce and mix thoroughly. Cover and cook over medium heat for 5 minutes, stirring occasionally. Stir and strain the tamarind water, discarding the solids. Add the tamarind water, garam masala and water to the crab, bring to a boil and simmer for 10 minutes.

BACHELOR'S CHICKEN CURRY
Kyethar Kalatharchet

This dish is a favourite of *kalathars* (bachelors) who, being too lazy to either buy a chicken or prepare a complicated curry, creep out into the night, steal a hen and throw it into the pot with a handful of spices. This version, for the "millennium bachelor", uses similar ingredients but follows a slightly more refined method of cooking. ☺☺

1 chicken, skinned and cut into eight pieces
1/4 teaspoon turmeric powder
1 teaspoon salt
1 tablespoon fish sauce
1 tablespoon ground ginger
1/4 cup (60 ml) oil
2 tablespoons minced onion
1 clove garlic, minced
4 dried red chillies, soaked and ground
1 teaspoon coriander seeds, dry-fried and ground
1 teaspoon garam masala
7 cm (3 in) cinnamon stick, broken in two
1 cup (250 ml) water

Score the chicken pieces and marinate in the turmeric powder, salt, fish sauce and ginger for at least 30 minutes. Heat the oil in a large pan, stir-fry the onion and garlic for 3–4 minutes then stir in the chilli paste and stir-fry for a further 2 minutes. Add the ground coriander seeds, garam masala, cinnamon and chicken and stir well. Cover and cook for 10 minutes, stirring frequently. Add the water, cover and bring to a boil. Reduce the heat to medium-low and simmer for 10–15 minutes, stirring occasionally.

Helpful hint: Prepare Indian breads, such as *chapati* or *naan*, with which to soak up the gravy or serve the curry with your regular choice of bread.

CHICKEN CURRY WITH TOMATO & CHICKEN AND GOURD CURRY

Kyethar Ngapichet & *Kyethar Buthee*

CHICKEN CURRY WITH TOMATO
🕐🕐🕐

1 chicken, cut into 8 pieces
1/4 cup (60 ml) oil
3 dried red chillies, soaked and ground
3 tablespoons finely sliced onion
1 teaspoon shrimp paste
1 tomato, deseeded and chopped
1 tablespoon finely sliced green chilli
1 cup (250 ml) water
12 g (1/4 cup) chopped saw-leaf herb, substitute
  coriander leaves (cilantro)

Marinade

1 tablespoon fish sauce
1 teaspoon salt
1/4 teaspoon turmeric powder
1 teaspoon ground ginger
3 cloves garlic, minced

Opposite:
Chicken Curry
with Tomato (left)
garnished with
saw-leaf herb;
and Chicken and
Gourd Curry
(right).

Mix all the Marinade ingredients together and combine with the chicken and set aside.

Heat the oil and stir-fry the chilli paste and onion for 5 minutes till fragrant. Stir in the shrimp paste. Add the tomato, green chilli and chicken, cover and cook for 5 minutes. Stir occasionally to prevent the chicken from sticking to the pan. Add the water, cover and cook over moderately low heat for 30 minutes till the chicken is done. Garnish with saw-leaf herb or coriander leaves.

CHICKEN AND GOURD CURRY 🕐🕐

A simple curry best served with plain rice.

4 chicken drumsticks, skinned
1/4 teaspoon turmeric powder
2 teaspoons ground ginger
1 teaspoon salt
2 tablespoons chopped onion
1 clove garlic, chopped
3 dried red chillies, soaked
2 tablespoons oil
2 tablespoons diced tomato
100 g (1 cup) bottleneck gourd, peeled, soaked
  for 10 minutes and cut into 10-cm-long
  (4-in-long) wedges
1 1/2 cups (375 ml) water

Score the chicken and marinate in the turmeric powder, ginger and salt for at least 10 minutes. Blend the onion, garlic and chillies to a paste.

Heat the oil and stir-fry the chilli paste till fragrant. Add the chicken and tomato. Cover and cook over low heat for 8–10 minutes, stirring occasionally. Add the gourd, cover and cook for a further 3 minutes then add the water and continue to cook for 30 minutes.

PAGAN PORK IN HORSE GRAM SAUCE
Wether Ponyegyi

Fermented Horse Gram Sauce is very popular among the people of Pagan, now known as Bagan, as it bestows a unique and intense flavour to meat and poultry dishes. ☺☺☺

500 g (1 lb) pork tenderloin, sliced
2 tablespoons Fermented Horse Gram Sauce
  (Ponyegyi, page 39)
1 teaspoon salt
1 tablespoon oil
3 tablespoons minced onion
1 clove garlic, minced
2 teaspoons chilli flakes
1 cup (250 ml) water

Marinate the pork in the Fermented Black Bean Sauce and salt for at least 30 minutes. Heat the oil in a pan and stir-fry the onion and garlic till fragrant. Add the chilli flakes and stir. Add the pork (spoon in all the marinade) and water. Cover and cook over medium heat for 30 minutes, stirring occasionally.

Helpful hint: Ponyegyi is available ready-made in Myanmar. Check Indian or Myanmar food stores for the ready-made product or follow the recipe for homemade Ponyegyi on page 39.

PORK BALLS COOKED IN SWEET SOYA BEAN SAUCE
Wether Ahchochet

The sweet and spicy soya bean gravy is a perfect match for the aromatic meatballs. Best served with plain rice and a vegetable dish such as Stir-fried Chayote (page 106). ☺☺

500 g (1 lb) minced pork
1 teaspoon ground ginger
3 cloves garlic, minced
1/2 star anise, fried and pounded
1 teaspoon salt
Egg white from 1 egg
2 tablespoons bread crumbs
1 cup (250 ml) oil, for deep-frying
3 tablespoons oil
1 tablespoon minced onion
1/2 teaspoon chilli flakes
1 tomato, diced
2 tablespoons sweet soya bean sauce
1 cup (250 ml) water
Pinch of salt, to taste

Garnishes
25 g (1/2 cup) chopped coriander leaves
   (cilantro)

Mix the minced pork, ginger, garlic, star anise, salt, egg white and bread crumbs in a large bowl. Knead thoroughly. Work the mixture into about 16 small balls, 2.5 cm (1 in) in diameter.

Heat the oil for deep-frying, add the pork balls. Deep-fry for approximately 10 minutes over high heat till golden brown.

Heat 3 tablespoons of oil in a saucepan and stir-fry the onion for 2 minutes. Add the chilli flakes and stir. Then add the tomato, pork balls, soya bean sauce and water. Cover and cook over medium-high heat for 10 minutes. Taste the sauce and add a pinch of salt if necessary. Garnish with the coriander leaves.

Helpful hint: For equally tasty beef balls, substitute minced beef for the pork and replace the star anise with 1 teaspoon ground cumin.

PORK AND MANGO CURRY
Wether Ahchin Chet

The degree of sourness in this pork curry depends very much on the mango used. Serve with plain rice, a vegetable dish and salad. ◑◑

500 g (1 lb) pork loin, cubed
1 tablespoon fish sauce
2 tablespoons oil
3 tablespoons minced onion
2 cloves garlic, minced
1 teaspoon ground ginger
3 dried red chillies, soaked and ground
1½ tablespoons peeled and shredded young
  mango
1 teaspoon salt
1¼ cups (300 ml) water

Marinate the pork in the fish sauce for at least 10 minutes. Heat the oil in a pan and stir-fry the onion and garlic for 5 minutes till fragrant. Add the ginger and chillies and continue to fry for 2 minutes. Stir in the pork, mango and salt and mix well. Cover and cook over low heat for 20 minutes, stirring occasionally. Add the water and simmer over low heat for 20–25 minutes.

Helpful hint: Young, or unripe, mango is recommended as it not only holds its shape better but also imparts a more pronounced flavour to the dish.

STEWED SORREL LEAVES

Chinbaung Gyawchet

Although it looks different, sorrel, also known as sour grass or roselle, is similar in taste and texture to the *chinbaung* leaves used in Myanmar. ◑◑

1 tablespoon shrimp paste
120 g (2 cups) well-packed *chinbaung* or sorrel
    leaves
3 tablespoons oil
1 tablespoon finely sliced onion
1 clove garlic, finely sliced
2 dried red chillies, soaked and pounded
3 tablespoons dried shrimp, soaked and ground
2 bird's-eye chillies, bruised
1 teaspoon salt
50 g (2 oz) bamboo shoots, cut into 7-cm long
    (3-in long) strips (optional)

Place a pan or wok over medium heat. Add the shrimp paste and sorrel leaves and dry-fry, stirring continuously, till the leaves are soft, almost to a paste. Remove from the pan and set aside.

Heat the oil in a pan and stir-fry the onion, garlic and chilli paste till fragrant. Stir in the ground dried shrimp, then add the bird's-eye chillies, sorrel leaves and salt, stir well. Add the bamboo shoots (if using). Simmer over low heat for 15 minutes or till a thick stew-like consistency is achieved, stirring occasionally.

SLOW-COOKED LABLAB BEANS

Pegyi Naut

This simple vegetarian dish offers a pleasant contrast of soft, melting beans and crisp, fried shallots and is delicious when eaten with Fried Dried Shrimp with Chilli (Balachaung Gyaw), page 38. ◍

1/4 cup (60 ml) oil
1/8 teaspoon turmeric powder
3 shallots, finely sliced
220 g (1 cup) dry lablab beans, soaked overnight and drained
1/2 teaspoon salt
1 cup (250 ml) water

Heat the oil in a pan, stir in the turmeric powder then add the shallots and fry till crisp. Remove the shallots and set aside. Add the lablab beans, salt and water to the shallot-infused oil, cover and cook over low heat for 30 minutes. Return the shallots to the pan about 5 minutes before the end of the cooking time.

STUFFED EGGPLANT & BAMBOO SHOOT CURRY

Khayanthee Naut & Myit Se Chet

STUFFED EGGPLANT

The vegetable is slow-cooked without much stirring, in order to keep it whole. ⓓⓓ

- 2 tablespoons oil
- 2 tablespoons minced onion
- 1 clove garlic, minced
- 2 dried red chillies, soaked and minced
- 1/4 teaspoon turmeric powder
- 1 teaspoon shrimp paste
- 3 tablespoons dried shrimp, soaked and blended to a powdery fluff
- 1/2 teaspoon salt
- 2–3 Asian eggplants
- 1/2 cup (125 ml) water

Opposite:
Bamboo Shoot
Curry (above) and
Stuffed Eggplant
(below).

Heat the oil and stir-fry the onion, garlic and chillies till fragrant. Stir in the turmeric powder and shrimp paste. Add the dried shrimp and salt and stir-fry for a further 2 minutes. Set aside.

Remove the stem from the eggplants. Hold each eggplant at the unsevered tip, insert knife 5 cm (2 in) from tip and slice lengthwise to the severed stem end. Give the eggplant a half turn and repeat so that there are 4 long wedges attached by the tip. Stuff the eggplant with the stir-fried paste. Transfer the stuffed eggplants to the pan used earlier and add the water. Bring to a boil, reduce the heat to low and cook for 25–30 minutes. Spoon the liquid over the eggplants and turn occasionally.

BAMBOO SHOOT CURRY

The spiciness of the chillies pairs well with the unique flavour of bamboo shoots. ⓓⓓ

- 1/3 cup (80 ml) oil
- 3 tablespoons ground onion
- 1/2 teaspoon ground ginger
- 1 clove garlic, ground
- 1/4 teaspoon turmeric powder
- 1 tablespoon fish sauce
- 1 tomato, diced
- 1 teaspoon shrimp paste
- 30 g (1/4 cup) dried shrimp
- 1 tablespoon chilli flakes
- 300 g (2 cups) bamboo shoots, sliced (drained if using canned bamboo shoots)
- 1 cup (250 ml) water
- 1/2 teaspoon salt
- 2 whole bird's-eye chillies, scored

Heat the oil over medium heat, stir-fry the onion, ginger, garlic and turmeric powder till fragrant. Add the fish sauce, tomato, shrimp paste, dried shrimp and chilli flakes. Stir-fry for 5 minutes. Add the bamboo shoots, water, salt and whole chillies. Cover and bring to a boil, then reduce the heat and simmer for 15 minutes.

STIR-FRIED BEANCURD AND BEANSPROUTS & STIR-FRIED CHAYOTE

Pepinpaukpepyar Gyaw & Gauyakharthee Gyaw

STIR-FRIED BEANCURD AND BEANSPROUTS

A light and tasty vegetarian dish which is fast to prepare and cook. Serve hot as an accompaniment to rice and meat dishes. ◷

- 2 cakes pressed (firm) beancurd cakes (about 300 g/10 oz), soaked
- 1/4 cup (60 ml) oil
- 1 teaspoon oyster sauce
- 1 clove garlic
- 240 g (3 cups) beansprouts
- 1/2 teaspoon salt
- 1 teaspoon cornflour, dissolved in 1 tablespoon water
- 1 teaspoon light soy sauce

Opposite:
Stir-fried
Beancurd and
Beansprouts
(above) and Stir-
fried Chayote
(below).

Drain the beancurd cakes and pat dry with paper towels. Slice each one in half then cut each half into 9 pieces to yield 36 cubes. Heat the oil, add the beancurd and deep-fry over medium-high heat for 5 minutes till golden on all sides. Remove with a slotted spoon and set aside. Retain 1 tablespoon of the oil for frying the vegetables, discard the rest. Heat the oil over high heat, stir in the oyster sauce and stir-fry the garlic. Add the beancurd, beansprouts and salt. Cover and cook for 3 minutes. Add the cornflour paste and soy sauce. Stir-fry for a further 3–5 minutes.

STIR-FRIED CHAYOTE

Chayote, also known as mirliton or christophene, is a sweet gourd that grows naturally throughout Myanmar. In this Chinese-influenced recipe, the freshness of the gourd is retained by fast cooking over high heat. ◷

- 125 g (4 1/2 oz) boneless pork, diced
- 1/2 teaspoon salt
- 1 teaspoon rice wine
- 1 tablespoon oil
- 3 cloves garlic, minced
- 200 g (2 cups) chayote, peeled, deseeded and sliced into 5-cm (2-in) strips
- 3 tablespoons water
- 1 teaspoon cornflour, dissolved in 1 tablespoon water
- 1 tablespoon light soy sauce
- Salt

Marinate the pork in the salt and rice wine for at least 10 minutes. Heat the oil over high heat, stir-fry the garlic and pork for 3 minutes till the meat is browned. Add the chayote and water and cook for another 5 minutes. Add the cornflour paste, soy sauce and a pinch of salt to taste. Stir-fry for another 5 minutes.

STIR-FRIED WATER SPINACH & STIR-FRIED KAILAN

Kazunywet Gyaw & Kailun Gyaw

STIR-FRIED WATER SPINACH

Variations on this recipe may be found throughout
the region. In Myanmar, water spinach is stir-fried
with fresh prawns and pungent shrimp paste. ☉

1 tablespoon oil
1 teaspoon shrimp paste
1 clove garlic, chopped
100 g (4 oz) fresh prawns, heads removed
2 whole bird's-eye chillies, bruised
1 teaspoon cornflour, dissolved in 1 tablespoon
   water
1/2 teaspoon salt
500 g (1 lb) water spinach, washed

Opposite:
Stir-fried Water
Spinach (left) and
Stir-fried Kailan
(right).

Heat the oil in a wok, stir in the shrimp paste. Add
the garlic and stir-fry till fragrant. Stir in the
prawns and continue to fry for 1 minute. Add the
remaining ingredients and stir-fry over high heat
for 3–5 minutes.

STIR-FRIED KAILAN

This simple recipe retains the crisp freshness of
kailan, a vegetable common to most of Southeast
Asia. ☉☉

125 g (1/2 cup) boneless chicken, cut into thin
   strips
1 teaspoon rice wine
300 g (5 cups) kailan, cut into bite-size pieces
1 tablespoon oil
3 cloves garlic
1/2 teaspoon salt
1 tablespoon light soy sauce
1 teaspoon cornflour, dissolved in 1 tablespoon
   water

Marinate the chicken in the rice wine for at least
10 minutes. Blanch the kailan in boiling water for a
few seconds. Heat the oil in a wok over high heat,
stir-fry the garlic and chicken for about 3 minutes
till the chicken is cooked through. Add the kailan
and cover for 30 seconds. Add the salt, soy sauce and
cornflour paste and stir-fry for 2–3 minutes.

VEGETABLES

SESAME-TOPPED SEMOLINA CAKE WITH COCONUT

Shwekyi Senyinmakin

This cake is usually served on festive occasions or when entertaining guests. The premier port city of Pathein (formerly known as Bassein), located in the Ayeyarwady delta, is particularly famous for this dessert. ☺☺☺

    240 g (2¹/₄ cups) semolina
    2¹/₂ cups (625 ml) coconut milk
    2¹/₂ cups (625 ml) water
    625 g (2¹/₂ cups) sugar
    2 teaspoons salt
    2 eggs, beaten
    ¹/₂ cup (125 ml) oil, heated
    75 g (¹/₂ cup) raisins
    2 tablespoons white poppy seeds

Preheat the oven to 200°C (400°F). Dry-roast the semolina in a frying pan over low heat for 10 minutes till reddish-brown, then cool. In a saucepan, add the roasted semolina, coconut milk, water, sugar, salt, beaten egg and hot oil. Bring to a boil and cook over medium low heat for 20 minutes till the mixture comes away from the sides of the pan. Stir continuously with a wooden spatula throughout the cooking process. If the mixture begins to stick to the pan, add a teaspoon or two of oil. Several minutes before the end of cooking, add the raisins and mix well.

Transfer the mixture to a lightly oiled round baking tray 30 cm (12 in) in diameter and 7 cm (3 in) deep. Smooth the surface with a metal spoon or cake knife and sprinkle the poppy seeds on the surface. Bake on medium shelf for 15 minutes. Remove from the oven and set aside for several hours at room temperature. Cut the cake in the baking tray and arrange the slices on a serving plate.

Helpful hint: As the semolina mixture thickens during cooking, it becomes increasingly difficult to stir. It is advisable to have someone else in the kitchen to assist with the stirring.

STICKY RICE WITH PEANUTS AND SESAME

Htamane

This sweet and filling dish is actually a snack that may be eaten throughout the day, usually with green tea. Traditionally, it is made for the rice harvest festival held in January or February. Almost every Myanmar household makes a dish of Htamane which may be shared among neighbours and offered to monasteries. ◑◑◑

1/2 cup (125 ml) oil
5 cm (2 in) fresh ginger, very thinly sliced into
   long strips
675 g (3 cups) uncooked glutinous rice, soaked
   overnight in water
1¼ cups (310 ml) water
2 teaspoons salt
100 g (1/2 cup) roasted peanuts, coarsely
   chopped
75 g (1/2 cup) sesame seeds
50 g (1/2 cup) shredded fresh coconut

Heat the oil over medium-high heat and, when hot, add the ginger and stir. After 30 seconds, add the drained rice, water and salt. Bring to a boil. Lower the heat and simmer for 20 minutes stirring occasionally. Add the peanuts, sesame seeds and shredded coconut. Remove the lid and continue to cook over low heat for 10 minutes while stirring and kneading the rice with a wooden spatula to soften the grains and prevent the rice from sticking to the pan. Drain the oil and transfer the rice to a plate.

Helpful hint: Be warned that kneading the glutinous rice can be very tough work and remember that during festival time in Myanmar this job is delegated to the menfolk.

FLOATING RICE DUMPLINGS

Mon Lon Ye Paw

These sugar-stuffed dumplings may be eaten for dessert or as a snack. During the Water Festival, mischievous girls stuff some of the dumplings with extra hot chillies. ⏱

  300 g (2 cups) glutinous rice flour
  150 g (1 cup) rice flour
  $^{1}/_{2}$ teaspoon salt
  $^{3}/_{4}$–1 cup (190–250 ml) water
  80 g ($^{1}/_{2}$ cup) diced palm sugar (substitute
    densely packed, soft brown sugar)
  8 cups (2 litres) water, to boil dumplings
  100 g (1 cup) freshly grated coconut

Mix the glutinous rice flour, rice flour and salt in a large bowl. Add the water a little at a time, mixing the ingredients thoroughly by hand. Continue to add the water and knead till a putty-like dough is achieved. Take care not to make the dough too soft. Take 1$^{1}/_{2}$ tablespoons of the mixture and roll into a ball. Flatten the ball slightly and make an indentation in the middle of the dough with your thumb. Place a little of the sugar in the indentation and fold the dough over it. Roll into a ball again. Repeat with the rest of the dough.

Bring about 8 cups (2 litres) water to a boil and gently place 5 or 6 balls into the water. The balls will sink initially. When they rise to the surface, they are cooked. Remove with a slotted spoon and drain. When all the dumplings are done, arrange on a plate and cover with the freshly grated coconut.

TRANSPARENT SAVOURY RICE PANCAKES

Ye Mon

More of an afternoon snack than a dessert, these deliciously light crêpes can be filled with a variety of different ingredients. ☉

300 g (2 cups) rice flour
2¹/₂ cups (625 ml) cold water
1 teaspoon salt
¹/₄ teaspoon baking soda
1 teaspoon finely chopped ginger
2 tablespoons oil
100 g (¹/₂ cup) cowpeas (garden peas may be substituted)
3 spring onions (green onions), sliced

Mix the rice flour, water, salt, baking soda and ginger in a bowl. Place a 30-cm (12-in) frying pan over medium heat and pour 2–2¹/₂ tablespoons of the rice paste into the pan. Lightly brush the pancake with a little oil and sprinkle on the cowpeas and spring onions (green onions). Cook for 3–4 minutes till the underside is crisp. Fold in half and cook for a further 1 minute on each side.

Helpful hints: As with crêpes, the choice of filling is many and varied. One popular savoury crêpe is filled with coarsely ground, toasted sesame seeds as well as peas and spring onions (green onions). Sweet crêpes, known in Myanmar as Mo See Kyaw, are filled with palm sugar, toasted peanuts, sesame seeds and coconut shreds.

STEAMED SWEETENED PEA DUMPLINGS

Mon Lakpya

Served warm, these desserts also make perfect high tea snacks. 🕐🕐

300 g (2 cups) rice flour
80 g (½ cup) diced palm sugar (substitute densely packed, soft brown sugar)
200 g (1 cup) cowpeas, boiled and pounded
1 cup (250 ml) coconut milk
1 teaspoon salt
2 tablespoons oil

Mix the rice flour and enough water to make a rice flour paste. Bring the palm sugar to a boil until reduced by half. Add the pounded cowpea and stir, continue cooking till the mixture becomes thick. Mix the rice flour paste, coconut milk and salt. Spoon 2 tablespoons or more of the rice flour paste on to a very fine cheese-cloth on a steamer.

Steam for 2 minutes before adding a tablespoon of the sweetened pea mixture. Fold the sides of the dough over the filling and steam for a further 2 minutes.

Index